BARRON'S DOG BIBLES

WITHDRAWN

German Shorthaired Pointers

Lani George and Joan Hustace Walker

D1530989

BARRON'S

Acknowledgments

The authors would like to thank Joan Tabor, not only for her introduction to the German Shorthaired Pointer but also for nearly two decades of "GSP" mentoring and friendship. Additionally, the authors (who are sisters) would like to thank their loving husbands and teenage daughters for their tolerance of a few late hours (okay, maybe more than a few...) and weekends spent writing while putting this book together. Additionally, Walker would like to extend a special thank you to Bob and Beth Ritchie of Robaron GSPs for their incredible generosity, time, and knowledge.

About the Author

Lani George has owned German Shorthaired Pointers for nearly 20 years. She has trained and handled her dogs to AKC conformation and field championships, as well as AKC hunt titles. Her first show champion, CH Tabor's Rock Solid, JH also competed successfully in National Shoot to Retrieve competitions, in addition to hunting geese in Canada and pheasant in the Dakotas. George is a lawyer and CPA, and has been published in various magazines and trade journals. She currently lives with her husband, two teenage daughters, a 15-year old GSP retired field champion, a future GSP puppy on the way, three horses, 22 chickens, and two dairy goats. (There used to be 25 chickens but George notes that the GSP is "old, not dead.")

Joan Hustace Walker is a multi-award winning writer and the author of more than 20 book titles. Walker's awards include seven Maxwell Awards and the AKC's Responsible Dog Ownership Public Service Award. She has been involved in the dog fancy for more than 30 years, and has competed with dogs from the Sporting, Working, Hound, and Toy breed groups, earning multiple titles. Though Walker previously owned an amazing GSP, she currently owns an elderly, rescued Rottweiler (12) and three Rottweiler-wannabe Havanese.

All information and advice contained in this book has been reviewed by a veterinarian.

A Word About Pronouns

Many dog lovers feel that the pronoun "it" is not appropriate when referring to a pet that can be such a wonderful part of our lives. For this reason, German Shorthaired Pointers are described as "he" throughout this book unless the topic specifically relates to female dogs. This by no means infers any preference, nor should it be taken as an indication that either sex is particularly problematic.

Cover Credits

Seth Casteel: front cover; Shutterstock: back cover.

Photo Credits

123rf: pages iii, 104, 121, 152, 161; Amber Johnson: page 148; Seth Casteel: pages 7, 10, 12, 18, 48, 51, 114, 168; Dreamstime: pages 58, 83, 167; Drsfostersmith.com: page 62; Cheryl Ertelt: page 63; Joan Hustace Walker: pages 20, 22, 24, 26, 29, 41, 45, 55, 66, 67, 75, 77, 82, 85, 107, 108, 111, 138, 145, 146, 150, 160; iStock Photo: pages 21, 50, 54, 68, 81, 117, 125, 127, 165; Daniel Johnson: pages 94, 96, 98, 132 (top), 132 (bottom), 133 (top), 133 (bottom), 134 (top), 134 (bottom), 135 (top), 135 (bottom), 136 (top), 136 (bottom), 137 (top), 137 (bottom), 142, 147; Liz Kaye: pages 11, 52, 171; Oh My Dog! Photography: page v; Shutterstock: pages i, vi, 2, 5, 8, 9, 14, 16, 30, 32, 34, 37, 39, 40, 53, 64, 70, 78, 86, 90, 93, 101, 116, 122, 129, 153, 158, 162, 163, 174, 178; Smartpakcanine.com: page 60; Kira Stackhouse: pages 155, 167.

All inquiries should be addressed to:
Barron's Educational Series, Inc.
250 Wireless Boulevard
Hauppauge, New York 11788
www.barronseduc.com

ISBN: 978-1-4380-7208-1 (Package)
ISBN: 978-0-7641-8678-3 (DVD)

Library of Congress Catalog Card No: 2012010559

Library of Congress Cataloging-in-Publication Data

George, Lani.
German shorthaired pointers / Lani George and Joan Hustace Walker.
p. cm. — (Barron's dog bibles)
Includes bibliographical references and index.
ISBN 978-0-7641-6490-3 (alk. paper)
ISBN 978-1-4380-7208-1 (alk. paper)
1. German shorthaired pointer. I. Walker, Joan Hustace, 1962– II. Title.
SF429.G4G37 2012
636.737--dc23
2012010559

Printed in China

9 8 7 6 5 4 3 2 1

CONTENTS

CONTENTS

PREFACE

The German Shorthaired Pointer was bred to be a versatile hunting dog. Of course, the qualities that have made this breed such an extraordinary gundog have also made him an athletic competitor in performance events, a winning show-ring exhibitor, a keen watchdog, and above all, a cherished companion. The GSP has always been a popular hunting dog; however, his versatility has made him an increasingly popular companion to active families.

The shorthair is not without his challenges, however. The GSP is a highly intelligent dog with a never-ending supply of energy and an intense focus on the job at hand, whether that job is learning a new obedience command, searching for chukar in dense undergrowth, diving into icy waters to retrieve a shot pheasant, charging through agility weave poles with truly amazing grace, or figuring out how to unlock the kitchen cabinet to reach a full garbage can inside.

For a new or prospective GSP owner, it is important to understand how that adorable, cuddly liver-and-white puppy will fit into your life. To successfully raise a GSP, it is important not only to understand the shorthair's strengths but also to have a good grip on what your biggest challenges will be in raising this sweet puppy. The GSP has been bred for very specific characteristics dating back to the late 1800s. These strong characteristics are what continue to make the shorthair such an outstanding, versatile hunting dog today. These same characteristics are also what can make a shorthair such a challenge to own, particularly if an owner doesn't understand the driving forces behind the shorthair.

The purpose of this book is present to you an honest guide to the German Shorthaired Pointer: his strengths, his challenges, his idiosyncrasies. And more important, how the shorthair's characteristics can translate into life as a companion dog, whether or not you intend to hunt your dog. If you are able to meet your shorthair's needs, which will involve lots of exercise as well as mental stimulation, your shorthair will reward you with the most precious gift he can give you: his undying loyalty.

This book will also walk you through your first days, weeks, and months of caring for and raising your GSP, as well as training tips, socializing him with people and other dogs, grooming information, health care, and tons of nuggets of GSP-specific information throughout. There's even a chapter specific to senior GSPs and a final chapter that will (we hope) pique your interest in hunting with your shorthair. Ideally, you will find this volume to be a resource to which you can refer throughout your shorthair's life.

Chapter One

All About German Shorthaired Pointers

The German Shorthaired Pointer, or "GSP" as he is commonly referred to, epitomizes the word *versatile.* With bloodlines dating back nearly 150 years, the GSP is adept not only in the field as a superb gundog, but also as an athletic performance dog, flashy show competitor, and highly trainable family pet. And when sufficiently challenged mentally and physically, at the end of a long day, the GSP can even be a suitable hearth and couch dog. The GSP's combination of amazingly sleek, good looks and the ability to be a do-all companion dog has this breed rocketing up the charts in popularity.

Origins of the GSP

As with many of the German breeds, the German Shorthaired Pointer developed from a need in the 1800s for a versatile or "all-around" hunting dog. Before the mid-1800s, hunting dogs were largely bred for single "game" purposes. Dogs were specialized for hunting waterfowl, upland birds, fox, deer, and wild boar. Depending on the type of game being hunted, some dogs were bred to hunt on land, others worked on water, and still others were bred specifically to hunt quarry underground. Hunting dogs were developed to track, retrieve, point, set, *or* flush but were not bred to possess all of these qualities at the same time.

Obviously, if a person wanted to hunt all types of quarry in all types of terrain (from open fields to dense underbrush and thick forests), he had to own many different types of hunting dogs. Until the mid-1800s, kennels of hunting dogs in the United Kingdom and Europe were typically owned by people of wealth (and usually a title). Hunting with dogs was primarily a sport, and only a person of some stature was able to financially support a kennel of hunting dogs (and the servants needed to maintain and care

1

for the dogs), as well as own a substantial amount of land that could be used for hunting. To ensure game was plentiful on his land and that no one poached any game, he often employed a gamekeeper and/or forester, too.

As Prussia's middle class became wealthier, and as more people had the means and were allowed to purchase or lease land, more people were able to own hunting dogs. Wanting to hunt an array of game, however, German hunters strove to develop an all-purpose, year-round hunting dog that could not only negotiate the range of weather and challenging terrain and forests found in Germany, but also find (scent), indicate (point), and retrieve game of both "fur and feather" on land and in water. The ideal, all-around hunting dog also had to be able to track wounded game, as nothing was to be wasted and it was against the thinking of the time to leave wounded game in the field.

Though commonly thought of as a dog of the middle class, the German Shorthair was appreciated by the ruling class in the 1800s, too. The favorite dog of the German emperor reportedly was a shorthaired German pointer named Waldin. "Waldin is of the purest blood, with a good pedigree, is brown in

Fun Facts

The first German Shorthaired Pointer club was founded in 1880 and called the Brown Tiger club. In 1891, the club changed its name to the Kurzhaar Berlin, with Dr. Paul Kleeman noted as the club's driving force and leading advocate. By 1897, the Kurzhaar Klub had 1,704 dogs listed in its registry. Today, the club is called the Deutsch-Kurzhaar-Verband e. V.

FYI: GSP Traits

The German word *Gebrauchshunde* was used in the late 1800s to describe the Shorthaired Pointer in Germany and means "adapted to all purposes" or an "all-around" dog. Interestingly, according to a German sportsman who was quoted in the 1891 edition of *The American Book of the Dog*, this included not only "retrieving hare or fox at a great distance, or to bring a duck out of the cold water and through thick woods, or to follow the trail of a wounded stag or roebuck," but also to perform guard work. The sportsman noted that the pointer who assists the government forester must not only be resistant to the range of forest temperatures but "must also, in case of need, render assistance to his master against game-sneakers, who frequently are a dangerous class of men, and often make a murderous attack on the officer when he interferes with their unlawful pursuits."

It is interesting to note that guarding abilities were also included in the original German breeders' ideal for the shorthair. In particular, it was noted that the breed should be able to perform the following:

- Guard against poachers
- Defend against predators

Though it's not discussed much, the shorthair of today can and *does* possess these qualities still, and at a minimum, today's GSP is an excellent watchdog that will sound the alert. Quite honestly, few would-be wrongdoers would enter a home with a shorthair in full guard mode—whether that dog would fiercely defend his home and family or simply lead the entrant to his jar of cookies. There is a basis for this guarding behavior in the GSP, and it's one pet owners need to be aware of so they can ensure that they properly socialize, in particular, those dogs that have more of a drive for guarding than others. (See "The Art of Socialization," page 71.)

color, and was whelped July 26, 1884. His nose is claimed to be equal to that of the best of English thoroughbreds. His figure is almost faultless, and his qualities first-class. He, like most German Pointers, is less nervous and restless than the English Pointers. He is not a one-sided field-trial dog, but a dog for all purposes—a 'Gebrauchshund.' … When partridge season opens, and the Emperor enters the field near Berlin to enjoy the sport of partridge-shooting, Waldin is always present, and the Emperor follows with delight the fine work of this dog."

Though the precise origins of the German Shorthaired Pointer of today are largely unknown, it is believed that German hunters in the early to mid-1800s used a combination of breeds to develop the foundation for the GSP. These breeds are thought to have included the Hannoverscher Schweisshund, the Old Spanish Pointer, the Old German Pointer, and the English Pointer. The English Foxhound, according to some sources, may have been used to slim the GSP's body and create a faster hunting dog.

As was true with the early stages of virtually all developing breeds in the 1800s and earlier, there were no breed guidelines. What this means is that

FYI: The GSP as a Military Dog

In a translation of the training of war dogs by the German Army (dated 1896), it was said that the most prized war dog was not the German Shepherd but the bird dog:

"Bird dogs, poodles and shepherd dogs are suitable for training for military purposes … Poodles are particularly esteemed on account of their docility, and they may therefore be employed for use for the purpose of instructing young trainers in the methods of training dogs. When old, however, they frequently lack interest in their work, and will often be found wanting in the accomplishment of the more severe tasks.

"The shepherd dog has in common with the poodle a high degree of intelligence; his ability of withstanding climatic influences, his watchfulness and attention to the orders of his master, would render him particularly suitable for use as a war dog were it not for the fact that in many cases his training is rendered difficult by his character, which is lacking in affection.

"The bird dog unites the good qualities of the foregoing two breeds and is distinguished by a lively sense of duty and attachment. His inclination for hunting is lost more and more as he becomes conscious that other things are required of him."

for the early German Shorthair (Deutsch Kurzhaar), each breeder used what dogs he saw fit to breed (and the bloodlines of breeds that were available to him) to create a versatile hunting dog. It wasn't until the establishment of the first Deutsch Kurzhaar club in Germany (1890) that a breed standard was established.

Before this time, German Shorthairs were bred for purpose (to be versatile hunters) as opposed to type (body style, color, head shape, and so on). Shorthairs in the 1800s were purported to include tri-colors, some with heavy bones, and others with shorter legs. When the German Shorthair breed club was formed in Germany, it sought to create a more consistent body type while maintaining the shorthair's hunting abilities.

According to the Deutsch-Kurzhaar-Verband e. V., the "father" of the GSP was a male German pointer named Hektor 1 (Stammb. Kurzhaar, Volume I, born 1872). This male pointer is credited as being the foundation used to build today's GSP. Of course, even Hektor 1 was quite different in appearance from GSPs even two decades later: The pointers at the time were often heavier, and had excessive throat skin, possibly a swayback, ectropion (a turning out of the eyelid), and soft paws. The earliest German pointers were considered slower and calmer workers that were highly efficient and outstanding retrievers.

By the early 1890s, period illustrations by noted German dog artist and cynologist Ludwig Beckmann (1822–1902) of the German "short-haired" pointer show a classic style and body type that is easily recognizable as edging toward the conformation of the GSP today. In the English translation of *Brehm's Tierleben,* by Dr. Alfred Edmund Brehm, Beckmann's illustrations include German Shorthaired Pointers in the plate: "Prize dogs of the International Dog Show in Hanover" (Hannover, Germany), which features two male GSPs, called Hector IV and Runal; and the plate titled "Prize Dogs of the International Dog Show at Cleve" (Kleve, Germany), which features a female GSP, Cora.

Fun Facts

The first two show championships awarded to German Shorthaired Pointers by the American Kennel Club went to dogs that were of Dr. Thornton's breeding.

In *The American Book of the Dog*, edited by G. O. Shields in 1891 (Rand, McNally & Company, 1891), an illustration of the German emperor's shorthaired pointer, Waldin, appears as illustrated by the German artist Heinrich Sperling (1844–1924). Though perhaps a bit heavier boned and lacking a bit of the elegance of today's GSPs, Waldin displays the great strides German breeders had made in only a few generations of breeding toward a more standardized "type."

War Years' Struggle

The advent of World War I in Germany dealt a crushing blow to German breeders. Food became scarce for Germans, not to mention their dogs. Breeders and entire lines of shorthairs are thought to have died during WWI. Records kept by breeders of other dogs in parts of Germany reported that dogs that made it through the war and didn't die in service, die of disease, or starve were often infertile.

The aftermath of World War II on Germany's purebred dogs was not much better. In fact, it has been reported that many breeders, wanting to protect their beloved dogs from the destruction of yet another war, sent them to other countries for safekeeping. Unfortunately, these dogs were sent to countries such as the former Czechoslovakia and Yugoslavia. After the devastation of World War II, many GSPs reportedly went home with Allied troops (both English and American) during the occupation in Germany,

further depleting the stock in the shorthair's native country but encouraging its spread in popularity across the world.

The Germans persisted, however, and through careful and diligent breeding, the Deutsch Kurzhaar slowly regained its foothold and is now the second most popular hunting dog in Germany.

Entry into the United States

The GSP's entry into the United States presumably could have been as early as the 1880s when German immigrants were making their way westward. These dogs, however, were not documented or noted with any registries (though there are pictorial records), so little is known about how many shorthairs may have come over at this time or what happened to them.

However, Dr. Charles Thornton of Missoula, Montana, is credited with importing Senta V. Hohenbruck in 1925, after reading about the Hohenbruck strain of GSPs in Austria. Senta arrived "in whelp" and delivered puppies on the Fourth of July, producing the first recorded litter of GSPs in the United States. Dr. Thornton went on to import 12 more GSPs from both Austria and Germany.

In addition to Dr. Thornton, several other Americans are credited with establishing GSP lines from imports during the same time period, including Ernst Rojem, Walter Mangold, and Joseph Burkhart. Geographically, in the early years, the GSP reportedly was most popular in areas such as Nebraska, Wisconsin, and Minnesota, where pheasant and chukar were hunted as opposed to the bobwhite, and the pointer was the bird dog of choice.

The AKC recognized the GSP as a breed in 1930, and in 1938, the German Shorthaired Pointer Club of America (GSPCA) was founded. In 1946, the club adopted the breed standard from the German club. As popular as the shorthair was with hunters, the breed did not begin to gain nationwide popularity until the 1960s. Though the GSP has never been in the top 10 among AKC registrations, it has been in the top 20 for many years and continues to hold steady as an American favorite.

Breed Truths

It's important to note that the *only* instance in which the black or black-and-white, roan, ticked, etc., GSP would be disqualified is in the show ring. A black GSP can be registered and compete and earn titles in all of the AKC's other performance events, such as hunt tests, field trials, agility, and obedience.

The Colors of the GSP

If you are purchasing a GSP in North America, you are most likely familiar with the liver-and-white shorthair. Depending on the way the white is patterned with the liver, the shorthair may appear "dark" (predominantly liver in color with flecks or ticks of white, for example) or "light" (much more white ticking is apparent and the liver appears more in patches). Of course, if

you spend enough time around shorthairs, you're sure to have seen the black coat variant.

The same color combinations that are found with liver can be found with black as the base (i.e., solid black, white with black ticking, and a black roan). Black and its color patterns are a disqualification in the show ring (conformation) in the AKC, the Canadian Kennel Club, and parts of Central America, but black and its color patterns are part of the allowed colors in standards written for the United Kennel Club (UKC), the FCI (the German standard that is used in Europe and most other countries), and what is considered the "British" standard (England, Australia, New Zealand, Singapore, Malaysia, Hong Kong, and so on).

Interestingly, black and its color variations (solid, ticking, and roan) are allowed with the German breed club, and these color combinations have reportedly been present since 1907, when German breeders Herr Bode and Dr. Waechter bred back to an Arkwright Pointer to improve pigment. In 1924, Herr Kleeman allowed the registration of "black" GSPs and their color variations as "Prussian" and with the designation Pr.K. In 1933, the German Club agreed to allow black GSPs into the studbook without the need for a designation.

Some breed historians speculate that the reason the black coloration was not included in the original AKC breed standard is that the GSPCA may have based its first breed standard on an earlier German standard that did not reflect the allowance of black color variants that occurred in 1933.

Very rarely seen but also present in the breed are little bits of "tan" (referred to as *Gelber Brand* in the German breed standard). The tan coloration has been present in the GSP for possibly 100 years; a German female, Atta Sand (b. 1921), was said to possess the tan color markings and was a littermate of the very famous German male shorthair Artus Sand. Technically, the presence of tan in a shorthair's coat would make the dog a "tri-color" (i.e., three colors: either tan, white, and liver; or tan, white, and black). The GSP with tan in its coat is not, however, a real "tri-color," in which the tan appears above the dog's eyes, on the muzzle, legs, and so on. (A good example of a traditional tri-color is the Bernese Mountain Dog or the tri-color Cocker Spaniel.) Tan markings are allowed with UKC and FCI (German) registries but are *not* allowed with the CKC, AKC, and the KC (Kennel Club)–and those that follow the American or British standards.

Breed Truths

Shorthair, Wirehair, Longhair?

Though developed in the same country, the German Shorthaired Pointer and the German Wirehaired Pointer are two distinct breeds. German Shorthaired Pointers can have long hairs in their coat; however, this is a severe fault in the breed ring. "Longhaired" pointers are not special, nor should they be considered more valuable, but if they are from a well-bred litter, they can make excellent hunting dogs and/or companions.

The following are descriptions of the colors and patterns found in the shorthair.

- **Solid liver:** Depending on the registry, this can be either a pure, solid, dark brown dog or a primarily liver dog with a small amount of white (or liver roan) on the chest or belly and/or the toes/paws.
- **Liver roan:** The base coat is liver with a very even mixture of white hairs in the coat.
- **Liver and white ticked:** This dog will appear to have a base coat of liver, which is a dark, rich brown color, and then will appear to have liver flecks or "ticking" throughout the parts of his coat that are white. (*Ticking* refers to the appearance of ticks in a dog's coat.)
- **Liver and white (no ticking):** This color combination is listed in the German breed standard and refers to a dog that does not have liver ticking in the white parts of his coat.
- **Liver spotted and white ticked:** *Spotted* in this reference is meant to represent larger patches of liver coloring (not small "spots" as you would find on a Dalmatian). The liver patches are often over the dog's eyes and ears, leaving a blaze of white on his face, and patches similar to saddle marks or on the dog's haunches; however, any and all placement of "spots" or patches is completely acceptable. In addition, this dog would have liver ticking throughout his white coat.
- **Black**, in all the color variants listed above.
- **Gelber Brand:** Any of the above colors and patterns with sandy-colored patches on face and/or paws.

German Shorthaired Pointers Today

The shorthair is one of the few breeds that has remained true to its roots and continues to be bred primarily for hunting (personal, hunt tests, or field trials). Even those breeders who focus on conformation are frequently involved in some working aspect of the breed.

What this means to the potential owner of a German Shorthaired Pointer is that this is not a dog that looks like a really cool hunting dog but is a calm, low-activity companion dog at heart. This is about as hard-core a hunting dog as it gets when it comes to hunting characteristics

Fun Facts

Celebrities with GSPs

Christy Turlington, model and actress, owns Klaus, a GSP.

The Hangover star Bradley Cooper rescued a GSP called Samson weeks before he was to be euthanized at a shelter. When Samson passed away, Cooper placed an enormous photo of him in his California home in tribute.

that are alive and well—even in dogs that haven't been bred specifically for hunting for several generations.

This is a highly intelligent working dog that thrives on mental stimulation and physical exercise. The pet home that can't meet this dog's sometimes demanding requirements is often faced with a supremely intelligent, high-performance gundog with intense hunting drives that without proper outlets for his intelligence and energy will end up presenting disastrous, destructive behaviors in the home.

If, however, a pet owner is able to meet or surpass the GSP's needs, the shorthair could possibly be the most amazing canine companion a person could ever hope to share his or her life with. The shorthair may be an intense dog in many ways, but that also means he is intensely loyal, and once a bond has been made with this dog, it is one that truly sets this breed apart from the others.

FYI: Docked and Undocked Tails

The issue of whether or not to dock a dog's tail has been a topic of discussion around the world, and in some countries, such as Australia, Belgium, Norway, Sweden, and Switzerland, and some provinces of Canada, docking is illegal. The concern is whether leaving a full tail on a hunting dog increases the potential for damage to the tail, or if the pain suffered when the veterinarian docks it is worse. Even with some tail left, GSPs can return from the field with horribly bloodied and torn tails. Though a full tail could provide a better counterbalance to the hunting dog, a full tail is also thought to be at greater risk for injury.

Docked tails are allowed in the United States, in many provinces of Canada, and in the United Kingdom and Germany, with provisions. In England, "working" dogs are allowed to have docked tails; however, show dogs only (those that are not actively hunted) must have a full tail. In Germany, all docking is prohibited for pups whelped in that country except for working gundogs. The docking styles vary from country to country, too. The "American" style leaves 40 percent of the tail remaining; "British" allows for 60 percent of the tail remaining, and the German (FCI) standard requires 50 percent of the tail remaining.

Chapter Two

The Mind of the German Shorthaired Pointer

The German Shorthaired Pointer is perhaps the most versatile of all hunting dogs, with an amazing array of qualities and characteristics that make him a skilled hunter of virtually all types of game. The GSP's medium size and terrific temperament make him a great fit in many different types of living situations—as long as his needs are met and his family understands how the breed's behaviors affect life in the home and backyard.

The World According to the GSP

The shorthair was bred to be a versatile hunting dog. What does this mean? Historically, hunting dogs had specific purposes: Each type of dog—setters, retrievers, spaniels, and pointers—had its own way of hunting and its own specific type of quarry that it hunted. If a person wanted to hunt all types of game, then he had all types of dogs. This was all well and good for the person who had his own game preserve and a warden to keep up the property and maintain a large kennel of hunting dogs. It wasn't so convenient for the less wealthy who needed a more well-rounded, do-it-all type of hunting dog.

The German Shorthaired Pointer was born from a desire to develop a dog that could do it all. The shorthair is capable of hunting upland birds, such as quail and pheasant, as well as mark the fall of a shot waterfowl and retrieve it from cold waters. Additionally, the GSP is adept at tracking injured birds, as well as hunting furred animals. The shorthair has the speed to be hunted on horseback, and the close-working ability to be hunted on foot.

This wide range of abilities has given the GSP a unique set of instincts, drives, and characteristics that are quite unlike other hunting dogs. For the pet owner, this translates into a dog that can be an equally amazing house pet; however, it is critical for the success of the GSP that his owners understand what the GSP's drives are, what motivates him, how he has been bred to respond, and how all this translates to living in a home with a family. When an owner understands why the shorthair behaves in certain ways, the owner can more easily meet the GSP's needs. Without a doubt, a happy shorthair means a happy owner.

What Makes the GSP a Great Dog

The German Shorthaired Pointer's list of positive qualities could stretch into an entire chapter. Enough good things cannot be said about this breed. Handsome, sleek, and strong, the shorthair is an attention-getter no matter where he is—whether running on the beach, strolling down the streets of Manhattan, gaiting in the show ring, or hunting in the thickest of undergrowth on an early, cold morning.

The shorthair's good qualities, of course, run much deeper than just good looks. This is a breed that is capable of being the most amazing companion you have ever owned. The same qualities that were necessary to make this breed the reigning versatile hunter translate into qualities that are much sought after for a canine companion.

Loyal The GSP loves his family. He wants to be in the middle of the action at all times. He is also not usually a "one-person" dog but rather loves all members of the family.

Hunter Extraordinaire Shorthairs have very strong hunting instincts. If there is a hunter in your family, the GSP is a primo choice for a personal hunting dog by weekend and family pet during the week.

Endurance The shorthair was bred to be tireless in the field. In the home, he is a great choice for the runner, the family with active older children, and those who enjoy hiking or other vigorous outdoor activities (that include the dog!). The GSP is also a great choice for owners who want to compete in performance events, such as agility.

Low Maintenance The GSP's short, dense coat is a favorite among hunters because it almost magically repels cockleburs, thorns, and other woodland "stickies" that can make grooming more feathered coats a nightmare. This coat quality makes the GSP an easy dog to groom, because virtually anything can be flicked off or wiped off. Shedding is minimal, too, as is odor.

Fun Facts

Just how versatile is the shorthair? Teams of GSPs have been used in sled-dog races, and individual dogs have been titled and/or awarded in such unusual sports (for a hunting dog) as Schutzhund and weight-pulling events.

Watchdog Abilities The shorthair, like many German breeds, was bred to be protective of his family and his home. He is *not* a guard dog, however. The well-socialized shorthair's ferocious barking stops immediately upon the owner welcoming the individual into the home. At that point, the GSP will greet friends coming into the home with great gusto.

Dog-Friendly Most hunting dogs were bred to hunt with other dogs. The shorthair is no exception to this rule and as a result, tends to be very social and playful with other dogs. This makes the GSP a favorite at dog parks and as a second dog in a family.

Breed Truths

Though the German Shorthaired Pointer can spend his days hunting in some extreme conditions, he is *not* a dog that can be left alone in the backyard. Mentally, this breed needs to be with his person or family and will do whatever it takes to make this happen, whether that is pulling off the back door to the house or jumping the fence and running around to ring the front-door bell. The GSP is happiest (and least destructive) as a house dog.

Soft-Mouthed It would not be to a hunting dog's benefit to have a hard bite; the prized pheasant would be shredded and wouldn't make for a good meal afterward. The GSP has a classic "soft mouth" for carrying birds with minimal damage. This means that the breed is often good around children, as it has good bite control.

Less Slobber The shorthair's mouth was designed for bird carriage and as such also does not have long flews. Though there are exceptions to every rule, in general this means that the GSP is not a big drooler.

Easy Housetraining The shorthair is noted for his ability to learn housetraining. With a reasonable schedule, a crate, and consistency, the shorthair can be reliably housetrained at a very early age.

Healthy Bred primarily as a hunting dog—and only more recently rising in popularity as a pet and personal companion—the shorthair enjoys a level of health not often seen in the top sporting breeds.

Intelligent The keen wit needed for the GSP to hunt both independently and under close command has created a supremely intelligent dog. The shorthair learns house rules quickly with consistent and positive training, and can be trained in multiple disciplines. One dog can be trained to perform agility, show in conformation, compete in obedience, hunt in the field, and retrieve in water—concurrently. This versatile intelligence is truly the hallmark of the GSP.

CAUTION

Never leave your shorthair unattended in the backyard. The GSP is a known escape artist and is quite capable of wriggling through, digging under, climbing over, or jumping a backyard fence. The lure of a rabbit on the "other side" can be all it takes for a shorthair to leave the yard and often not return willingly.

Challenges of Owning a GSP

Of course, generations of breeding for a versatile hunting dog has created instincts, drives, and characteristics in the GSP that can be challenging for some pet owners. Basically, the challenges of owning a GSP as a pet occur when an owner is unprepared for issues that can develop when a hunting dog doesn't hunt. Taking a dog that was bred to run all day in the field in a constant search for game, and placing him in a home with a fenced backyard and children running about, creates a different scenario for the shorthair. None of these challenges is insurmountable; however, an owner needs to be aware of how a GSP could behave in the home and how best to solve these challenges.

Bore Easily The benefit of owning an exceptionally intelligent dog is often a double-edged sword. It makes training much easier; however, it also means that this dog will become bored easily. If the shorthair is not mentally challenged throughout the day (via constant interaction with his owner, the use of interactive toys and chews, obedience training, long walks and jogs, and so on), he will find ways to amuse himself, from figuring out how to open drawers, cabinets, doors, and the refrigerator, to destructive behavior based on serious mental frustration.

Headstrong The strong hunting instinct that serves the GSP so well in the field can also lead to an unwillingness to obey commands that the shorthair knows well. Specifically, recalls can be challenging to train with great consistency—particularly when out in an open field: "Excuse me? You obviously didn't mean to call me when I can smell a rabbit trail! Are you serious?"

Fun Facts

True story: A young female GSP learned to open the refrigerator door. The owners had to bungee the refrigerator doors to keep their shorthair from regularly treating herself to leftovers. Never underestimate the mental powers of a bored shorthair!

High Energy So, take a dog that is capable of running all day and put that dog in a house 24/7. If not given ample exercise (i.e., a hard, daily run at the dog park; a hard, daily run with the owner; or both), the shorthair will be out of control. The dog is not hyper (energy without focus), but he could appear this way if he is expected to bottle up his activity level. He will also try to burn off energy by doing not-so-terrific things around the home, such as digging massive holes in the yard; running hell-bent through the house; shredding pillows; shredding furniture; shredding rugs. . . . You get the idea. Regular exercise is a must with this breed—for everyone's sanity.

Breed Truths

For a breed with such a soft mouth, the GSP is capable of wreaking destruction on pillows, stuffed toys, and furniture. Anything with a soft inside apparently needs immediate gutting, but never in the presence of the humans in the home. This shredding habit can be dangerous to the GSP, because the fluffy insides can choke the dog or create a dangerous gastrointestinal blockage.

Coat Oil Bred to be able to retrieve birds from cold waters, the shorthair has a certain amount of oil in his coat. This oil can make bathing frustrating (the water runs off the surface as if the dog has an invisible raincoat), but if the dog is not bathed with some regularity (every month or so is more than enough), the buildup of oils can create a "doggie" smell that some may not find particularly pleasant.

Prey? In addition to being a stellar bird dog, the shorthair is quite capable of hunting rabbits and other small, furred animals. This can create a challenge to homes with a cat. Some shorthairs will never respect a cat; others, if raised as a puppy with a cat, may live peacefully with the feline. It can happen, but it often doesn't.

Mouthy As discussed previously, GSPs were bred to have soft mouths to retrieve game without damaging the meat. They can also be a bit "mouthy" in that they will grab and hold a person's hand, foot, appendage, and so on. This can easily be corrected with simple behavioral training (if the GSP pup has a toy in his mouth, he can't put your hand in his mouth), but it is a trait among hunting dogs that is more pronounced than in other breeds.

Dribblers Shorthairs are not droolers, but they are dribblers. Is it a game to see who can make the longest water trail across the room from the water bowl after drink-ing? It's hard to say, but it is strongly suggested that an owner get used to the sloppy drinking and put a towel under the water bowl.

Breed Truths

The shorthair is not a dog that typically challenges your leadership on a daily basis; however, as with any breed of dog, it is important to establish the rules early and enforce them consistently with kind and firm guidance. Obedience training is a must.

COMPATIBILITY Is the GSP the Best Breed for You?

ENERGY LEVEL	● ● ● ● ●
EXERCISE REQUIREMENTS	● ● ● ● ●
PLAYFULNESS	● ● ● ●
AFFECTION LEVEL	● ● ● ●
FRIENDLINESS TOWARD CATS/SMALL MAMMALS	●
FRIENDLINESS TOWARD OTHER DOGS	● ● ● ●
FRIENDLINESS TOWARD PEOPLE	● ● ● ●
WATCHDOG ABILITIES	● ● ● ● ●
FRIENDLINESS TOWARD CHILDREN	● ● ● ●
EASE OF TRAINING	● ● ● ●
GROOMING REQUIREMENTS	●
SHEDDING	● ●
SPACE REQUIREMENTS	● ● ●
OK FOR BEGINNERS	● ● ●

5 Dots = Highest rating on scale

Rambunctious This high-energy hunter loves his people and will enthusiastically seek out attention. Because of his stalwart build and size, he is adept at bowling over children and unsteady adults as he scrambles for attention and pats. Though this enthusiastic dog has the best of intentions (remember, he *loves* his people), it can be intimidating to young children or those who are unsure around dogs. Regular exercise and training alternate behaviors for attention can easily tamp this wild greeting behavior. (There's nothing more fun—and impressive—than to see a wildly wriggling grown GSP skid into a *sit* from across the floor to receive pats!)

Breed Needs

Singles, young couples, and empty-nesters need to carefully consider how the addition of an active, demanding, and intelligent dog will affect their lifestyles. If long hours at work are the norm, if you enjoy going out after work, or if you travel frequently, you'll need to determine if you can (and are willing) to adapt your lifestyle to your shorthair's needs.

Bed Buddies You'd think that a dog trained to work so hard in the field would be content to lie on a hard floor beside your feet. He's a working dog, right? Ha! The GSP has an uncanny knack for finding the softest bed or couch in the house (preferably one currently occupied by a family member to snuggle up with) and will largely ignore the stylish, expensive dog bed you just bought him.

Separation Anxiety When a dog is bred to work alongside his master all day long, this translates into a dog that wants to be with his owner all day long. The GSP bonds intensely with his family. Unfortunately, this also means that the shorthair can develop severe separation anxiety—to the point of being dangerous to himself even when crated. Much can be done to help prevent severe separation anxiety (see page 58); however, many GSPs will require crating when the owner is gone to prevent injury to themselves and frantic destruction to the home.

Helpful Hints

If your GSP is an "only" dog, it is important to socialize him with other dogs as he grows up. Dogs can get "rusty" in their friendly dog behavior—both in displaying appropriate behaviors and reading other dogs' intentions—and regular meet-ups with other age-appropriate playmates is important for growing pups and young adult dogs.

GSPs as Family Dogs

The GSP's history of being bred to work with people translates into a dog that has an exceptionally strong desire to be with people. There is no dog better suited to being a family dog than one that sincerely wants to be with people. Additionally, the shorthair is not a breed that bonds strongly with one person (and ignores the rest of the family). Rather, the shorthair tends

to love his entire family, showing no real favorites (though there is usually someone he recognizes as the "leader" of the family pack).

The most problematic issue with a GSP in a young family is the breed's tendency to be boisterous with his affections. He never intends to hurt anyone, but because of his sheer strength, speed, and athleticism, he can easily bowl over small children, trip up teens, and knock over a frail adult. Obedience training (see Chapter 7) is a *must* for this breed to behave appropriately in the home; however, even the well-trained GSP can sometimes just get too excited when he recognizes a favorite visitor and temporarily forgets his rock-solid training.

Exercise is another must for the GSP to succeed as a family dog. With a good run at the dog park, a long jog with a family member, or several walks during the day (and a high-speed game of fetch in the backyard), the "edge" will be off the shorthair and he'll be more apt to listen to commands and willing to greet family members a little more carefully. With that said, even the well-exercised GSP will immediately spring into high-speed play mode if he sees young kids running and screaming through the house or teens engaged in a wrestling match.

Perhaps the most important question a family needs to ask is, Do we have the time to meet the needs of the German Shorthaired Pointer? A busy family that is constantly on the go with one or more children involved in soccer practice, baseball games, music lessons, swim meets, tutoring sessions, and so on may find it difficult to carve out enough time for the shorthair's attention, exercise, and training requirements. The family that can do this—or better yet, do this *and* integrate the puppy or adopted adult into their busy lives—has the greatest chance for success.

CAUTION

Shorthairs cannot be trusted in the home with birds or small mammals that are being kept as pets. Regardless of type or size of bird, your GSP will see it as natural prey. Small mammal pets, such as house rabbits, guinea pigs, chinchillas, and ferrets, are also "game." Both fur and fowl will be hunted ... relentlessly. It doesn't matter if the bird or small mammal is kept contained in a different room, the shorthair will *never stop hunting* the creatures. This can lead to extreme frustration for the dog, a life of terror for the bird or small mammal, complete and utter destruction of anything that lies between the dog and the bird or small mammal, and guaranteed insanity for the owner.

And do not think that the cage is enough to protect the bird or small mammal. It isn't.

With Other Pets

The shorthair was bred to work with other dogs in the field and is actually trained to "honor" another pointer's "find" if the other dog found the game first. As a result of generations of breeding for a hunting dog that can get along with other dogs in a highly competitive situation

(these dogs *live* to find birds), GSPs are generally quite dog-friendly. A shorthair puppy that is introduced into a home that already has a resident dog generally settles into the family quite well. Whether the older dog bonds with the younger pup or would rather ignore the newcomer is dependent on the individual dogs' temperaments. (See page 81 for tips on introducing the "second" dog.) Usually, however, adding a shorthair to the home—whether you already have a shorthair or have another breed—is not a problem.

If socializing at the dog park is going to be a regular staple in your dog's life (it's a great way to get that important exercise in every day!), the shorthair is often a park favorite. Shorthairs are typically quite friendly with other dogs—regardless of size, shape, coat, or color. Their manner of play is not offensive to other dogs, and their play behaviors and body language are very "readable" by virtually all other breeds.

If you plan to introduce your shorthair into a family with a cat, be forewarned that this may or may not be successful. GSPs are *not* known for their friendliness toward cats and more often see the cat as furred prey. An owner may have success introducing a shorthair to a cat with very careful introduction and if the shorthair is a puppy. Growing up with a feline has been successful with some GSPs; however, all bets are off if the cat is outside and takes off running.

Some adult GSPs coming out of rescues have also been placed successfully with cats in a home; however, this is the exception and definitely not the rule!

The Importance of Exercise with the GSP

Yes, it has been rumored that there are German Shorthaired Pointers in the world that are content to lounge on the couch all day and require little to no exercise. These shorthairs are generally either quite advanced in age, suffering from a thyroid deficiency, or poseurs (not really GSPs). All kidding aside, shorthairs are high-energy dogs with incredible stamina. This is what they were bred for and why they are such amazing, versatile hunting dogs.

Exercise is critical for this breed. Not only does it provide physical stimulation, but it tends to take the "edge" off the shorthair. The well-exercised adolescent and adult dog is far less likely to challenge his owner. Regular exercise away from the dog's home (such as running at a dog park, hunting at a dog club, jogging at a local park, or walking in the neighborhood) tends to lessen the dog's territorial aggression (a good thing).

A well-exercised dog is often more relaxed, is less likely to experience separation anxiety (more on this on page 58), and tends not to show as many destructive behaviors (from boredom and/or pent-up energy). The relaxed dog is better able to focus on training exercises, too. In short: A tired shorthair is a *good* shorthair.

Putting It All Together

The German Shorthaired Pointer is an amazing dog. He is exceptionally devoted to his family, exceedingly intelligent, and eager to please. If you can meet this breed's exercise needs and training requirements, he could be the best dog you've ever owned. If the energy requirements of an adolescent or young adult dog are too much for you but you really love this breed, consider adopting an older adult shorthair.

If you're uncertain whether the GSP is really the dog for you, contact the German Shorthaired Pointer Club of America (see "Resources," page 169) and speak to breeders in your area. Visit with the breeders' adult dogs and ask questions about how best to integrate this type of dog into your home. Many breeders will give you referrals to people they have sold their puppies to—this is a great resource. Ask these new puppy owners what problems they've had to work through with their shorthairs.

Additionally, consider contacting a regional chapter of the National German Shorthaired Pointer Rescue (see "Resources," page 169). Those involved in rescue will give you the unvarnished truth about why so many shorthairs fail in pet homes (hint: It's not the dog's fault) and are exceptionally helpful in figuring out how to modify your home and lifestyle to accommodate the needs of the GSP.

As you might have gleaned, the shorthair is not the dog for everyone, but when his owner understands his natural drives, characteristics, and hunting nature, he can be a fantastic companion for many people.

Chapter Three

How to Choose a German Shorthaired Pointer

How do you choose between energetic, bouncing, licking (and completely adorable) liver-and-white puppies? What do you need to know to make the best choice for your planned activities and your home? The best puppy for you will depend on a puppy's background and breeding, as well as your expectations for the GSP as an adult.

It is important to know what you're looking for before beginning your search. Your new GSP will have the best chance of succeeding if he most closely fits both what you want in a dog (activity level, temperament, health, and looks) and what you can afford as far as time and effort.

GSP Choices

First, are you completely set on getting a puppy? Yes, they are absolutely adorable, but they are a lot of work for the first three or four years in the home, and can be utterly destructive. Contrast this with an adult dog that may already have some training, may be housetrained, and is ready to jump into a family routine with love and kisses.

The average life span of a GSP is 10 to 12 years. If you adopt a six- or seven-year-old dog, you will still have many years of companionship and fun together. There are lots of dogs given to shelters and rescues all the time, so you may be able to find that perfect companion in one of these dogs.

If an adult might be the best fit for your family or if you would like to learn more about the adopted GSP, see "The Adoption Process" on page 45. If you are considering purchasing a shorthaired puppy, read on!

PERSONALITY POINTERS
Who's the Sweetest of Them All?

Each GSP is truly an individual. Some are quiet and regal; others seem determined to drive the average person crazy. In general, though, GSP males tend to be very affectionate and the type to follow you everywhere you go. Females love attention, too, but are a bit more independent and can be content to snooze in their own corner for a while.

Field and Show Lines

When looking for a GSP breeder, you will probably hear a lot of different terms used to describe the breeding, or lines, behind a given litter of puppies. Breeding for a particular purpose tends to result in dogs with certain instincts or conformation. Champion-to-champion breeding, however, does not guarantee champion offspring. Every puppy is an individual, with different abilities, temperament, and looks.

Breed Truths

Because the German Shorthaired Pointer was bred to hunt virtually everything, some of them can be very aggressive toward cats. Severe cat aggression is not an instinct that can be trained "out" of an adult dog. Though a pup that is raised with cats may fare well with cats in the home, it is also entirely possible that if the pup sees cats as something to be hunted, he and a pet cat may *never* be safely left alone. Bird owners should also be aware that it is the exception to the rule in the world of intensely focused, bird-hunting GSPs for a dog to live peacefully with a bird.

For example, a puppy bred for field trials may be an amazing personal hunter but may not have the run or nose for success in the highly competitive world of field trials. A puppy bred for show may be gorgeous but may not quite have the conformation to win. Likewise, a puppy bred for hunting may be able to be shown in conformation, and a puppy bred for the show ring may be excellent in the field. It is a hallmark of the breed that the majority of GSPs can still hunt, even though they may not have been bred specifically for the field.

Totally confused yet? Don't be. The GSP is the do-it-all dog. There are some breeders who choose to focus more heavily on one part of that total picture. As noted above, typically breeders are divided into two groups, field and show.

Here's an explanation of what is meant by field and show lines, and how purchasing a puppy from either one of these lines (or a combination of both field and show) translates into its potential as a family pet, personal hunter, performance event competitor (such as agility, rally, or flyball), show dog, house dog, and any combination thereof.

Field Lines

Historically, all German Shorthaired Pointers were bred for hunting in the field. Although most people when they think of "hunting" tend to think of upland bird hunting, the GSP was bred to do it all: retrieve waterfowl from coldwater ponds, streams, and marshes in a manner similar to Labrador retrievers; hunt and retrieve upland birds in dense, thick underbrush as the pointer was bred to do; track furred game, such as rabbit, but without the "tongue" of Beagles; track wounded large game, such as deer, which is a job classically performed by Dachshunds; drive off vermin, a job typically noted as belonging to the terrier group; and bark at home intruders, at times showing protective characteristics normally considered reserved for guarding breeds.

Some lines, however, are bred specifically for field-trial competition, which in the United States means the GSPs from field lines are bred to hunt upland birds and hunt these birds in a competitive manner. Translated, those who breed specifically to compete in field trials with their GSPs focus their breeding on very specific traits. To win at field trials requires a dog with a great deal of "run," boldness, intensity, style, and perfect manners.

Distinctive (and necessary) for a competitive field-trial dog is the critical characteristic of good "run." A dog with good "run" is one that hunts at full speed, shooting down tree and brush lines at distances from a half mile to a mile away from the handler. During competition, the dogs are often out of sight, and handlers (who are generally mounted on horseback but can handle

from foot) typically use a mounted scout to help track where the dog is. You don't want to ride right past your dog if he is locked on point, after all!

In a field trial, the dogs run for 30 minutes (up to 45 minutes or 60 minutes at national-level events). Needless to say, a dog that has the stamina and energy to perform at this level has a lot of energy. If this energy is not spent running in the field, it will be spent doing something else.

What does this mean to the pet owner? The GSP is already considered a high-energy breed with an above-average requirement for exercise and mental stimulation. The field-trial dog is the Olympian of speed and endurance in hunting. There are always exceptions to the rule, and dogs with less drive and run do appear in every litter; however, a hearth dog is not the goal of the breeder who is focused on producing competitive field-trial dogs.

With that said, if you are interested in the competitive world of field trialing, you will want to seek out a top-notch GSP breeder who breeds for and actively competes in field trials. If you have a keen interest in hunting (personal, versatile, hunt tests, and so on) a field dog may also be an excellent choice.

Breed Truths

Both show and field lines from high-quality breeders generally enjoy good health, as high-quality breeders—whether they focus on show or field—hold good health as one of their top priorities and test for hereditary diseases.

Pet owners seeking a companion dog may consider a GSP from field-trial lines if they have physically active lives themselves and if they plan to include their GSPs in these activities. The field GSP can be a great companion for runners and joggers who want to run with their dogs. Do you like to spend your weekends hiking, climbing, and/or camping with your dog? A field dog will keep up with you and then some. Pet owners who enjoy competitive sports, such as agility, flyball, rally, and other performance events, may also be interested in field lines, though a GSP from show lines will also have plenty of energy for these activities.

Basically, if the pet owner can meet the field dog's daily physical and mental needs, the GSP from field lines may be a good fit.

In addition to a faster, more intense hunting style, the build of some GSPs from field lines is slightly different from that of a GSP bred for show and general hunting. Because the field dogs are bred for hunting characteristics and speed, they tend to be a little smaller and a bit leaner than those bred for show and personal or versatile hunting. Some field GSPs also have a much more erect, "hard" tail carriage when on point. Though this looks particularly flashy, this carriage (which is fine in the field) is actually a fault in the show ring, where the preferred tail carriage is more of a 45-degree angle.

As you can see, the difference between field lines and show lines within the GSP breed is very subtle and is not as markedly pronounced as in other sporting breeds. This is principally because GSP breeders continue to value the versatile hunting dog.

Show Lines

People who breed for the show ring seek to breed dogs that express the breed standard as closely as possible. The breed standard is considered to be perfection in body, movement, and temperament and was written to best describe the characteristics and qualities of the perfect, versatile hunting GSP. As noted previously, unlike some sporting breeds where there is a distinct separation between those who show their dogs and those who hunt their dogs, most GSP show breeders value the breed's hunting characteristics, because these breeders hunt or compete in hunt tests with their own dogs. Therefore, the hunting instinct is still present in most show dogs. You will often see show dogs at AKC hunting tests or versatile tests, and sometimes at field trials.

Show lines tend to be taller and heavier than field lines. (A personal hunter/show dog does not need to be as hard and lean as the field-trial dog.) A show dog will tend to hold its tail at a graceful, 45-degree angle when on point (the "classic" position), whereas, some field dogs will often hold their tails vertically, in a hard, erect position (an angle that would be penalized in the show ring).

ACTIVITIES Titles Explained

Titles indicate a dog's accomplishments. Your puppy's pedigree will reflect three generations of GSPs before him and all that they've achieved. Here is a list of some of the titles you might see on your pup's pedigree and what they represent. Titles that come before a dog's name (these titles require winning against other dogs):

CH	Champion (show/conformation)
NSC	National Specialty Champion (winner of the GSPCA's National Specialty Show)
FC	Field Champion (field trial)
DC	Dual Champion (combination title, usually in show and field)
AFC	Amateur Field Champion (field-trial champion handled by an amateur)
NFC	National Field Champion (winner of the breed national field trial)
NAFC	National Amateur Field Champion (winner of the amateur-handled division of the breed national field trial)

Titles that come after the dog's name (these titles require meeting certain performance requirements):

JH	Junior Hunter (entry-level hunt test)
SH	Senior Hunter (intermediate-level hunt test)
MH	Master Hunter (advanced-level hunt test)
CD	Companion Dog (entry-level obedience)
CDX	Companion Dog Excellent (intermediate-level obedience)
UD	Utility Dog (advanced-level obedience)
NA	Novice Agility (AKC)
OA	Open Agility
AX	Agility Excellent

Show dogs are not bred specifically to compete in field trials but are considered quite suitable for less hard-running hunting competitions or as a close, personal hunter, and as such may be less high-energy and less demanding of hard, daily exercise as an adult than a field dog. This does not mean that you can reasonably expect a GSP from show lines to be a couch potato or hearth dog before the age of 12. Regardless of field or show lines, the GSP remains a high-energy dog that requires a lot of exercise, and the potential GSP owner should be prepared to meet these needs.

Both show and field breeders sell to pet owners! In fact, it is estimated that in an average, well-bred litter, anywhere from 20 to 80 percent of the puppies go to pet homes. Pups with outstanding potential will be sold to those seeking a dog with show or field potential; however, the remaining pups will go to pet homes, where the pet owner receives all the benefit of the breeder's hard work in developing healthy, athletic dogs with great temperaments.

Dual Lines

Some GSP breeders, like their dogs, "do it all." These breeders strive to breed dogs that can compete in both show and field. Even with the perfect GSP, earning a dual championship is exceptionally difficult and a huge investment of time and money for the breeder, as both trialing and showing include the commitment to extensive hours training in the field, experience handling in the show ring, time and expense traveling to competitions, money spent for entries, possible expenditures for professional training and show handling, and so on. Despite this, German Shorthaired Pointers have one of the highest rates (if not *the* highest rate) of "dual champion" sporting-breed dogs in the AKC breed registry.

Fun Facts

Perhaps one of the most famous dual champions (DC) among GSPs is BIS/BISS/NSC Can Ch DC NMK's Brittania V. Sibelstein, HOF. "Brit" finished her career with a record-setting 49 Best in Show (BIS) wins, 141 Sporting Group First placements, 14 BISS (Best in Specialty Show), and overall winner at a GSPCA National Specialty Show (NSC). Brit's wins included back-to-back Sporting Group First wins at the Westminster Kennel Club dog show.

FYI: What's a CHIC Number?

The GSPCA recommends that GSP breeders test their dogs for certain genetic diseases and register the results of these tests with the Canine Health Information Center (CHIC). For test results to be registered, the dog must have a form of permanent identification, such as a tattoo or microchip, and the health tests must be performed or the exam evaluated by the specific organizations and/or specialists outlined by the GSPCA on the CHIC web site. Note that just because a dog has had the tests performed and the results have been registered with CHIC (and the dog has received a CHIC number), this does not mean the dog is clear of these diseases. It does mean that given the dog's CHIC number, you can look up the dog's results.

Who Is a High-Quality Breeder?

Whether you're looking for a field-bred GSP or one from show lines, the key to finding a great German Shorthaired Pointer puppy, one that meets your expectations of what a great GSP should be, is finding an excellent breeder. But who exactly is a great breeder?

Involved in Dog Sport: Reputable, knowledgeable breeders are typically involved in some way in the sport of dogs. They could be very involved in the show ring with some involvement in the hunting world, such as hunt tests. They could be involved primarily with versatility and compete in multiple performance events, as well as hunting with their dogs. Or, their breeding program could focus primarily on field-trial championships.

If a GSP breeder is not involved in some aspect of dog sport—show or field—then this is a red flag to any potential puppy buyer. It is only by working with these dogs that a person can have a true appreciation for what is correct in the breed and what is not.

Participate in Breed and/or All-Breed Clubs: High-quality breeders also are involved with a local, regional, and/or national breed club in conformation and/or field. Whether the breeder's focus is more on show or field, he or she is still focused on improving the breed. Involvement in a club shows the dedication of the breeder and his or her involvement in the best interests of one or more facets of the GSP.

Support Breed Rescue: High-quality breeders are involved and support breed rescue. They will take back their dogs for any reason at any time. (Note: This does not mean you will get your money back! This means that the breeder is determined that none of his or her dogs will end up in shelters or pounds if they are unwanted.)

Test and Certify Health: The high-quality breeder strives to produce the healthiest dogs possible. The GSP tends to be a healthy breed, but it is

CHECKLIST

Red Flags

The breeder you may be talking to could be less than reputable if:

✔ the breeder wants to meet you somewhere other than his or her home to sell the puppy (such as a flea market, a rest stop off the highway, someone else's home, out of the back of his or her pickup truck, and so on).

✔ the breeder doesn't ask any questions about you other than how you'd like to pay for the puppy.

✔ the breeder accepts credit cards.

✔ the breeder will ship anywhere without knowing anything about the pup's future home.

✔ the breeder says his or her dogs are healthy and don't need any health tests.

✔ the breeder sells (and ships) puppies that are younger than eight weeks.

✔ the breeder raises and sells several different breeds of dogs.

✔ the breeder is not involved in any performance, hunting, or conformation events and belongs to no local, regional, or national dog clubs.

✔ the breeder specializes in "rare" colors of GSPs. (The black coat color variant of the GSP is not rare. This coloration can be registered with the AKC, but it is not desirable and is a disqualification in the show ring.)

not without health concerns and is at risk for several debilitating and/or fatal genetic diseases. High-quality breeders are open about the issues they have had in their lines and will discuss what they test for and the results of all of their dogs. At a minimum, the breeder should have a CHIC (Canine Health Information Center) registration number that confirms the GSP has been tested for the following:

• Congenital Cardiac Disease (Orthopedic Foundation for Animals—OFA—evaluation with exam performed by either a veterinary cardiologist or a veterinary specialist)
• Hip Dysplasia (OFA or University of Pennsylvania Hip Improvement Program—PennHIP—evaluation)
• Progressive Retinal Atrophy (Canine Eye Registration Foundation—CERF—evaluation, annually until age six; every other year afterward)
• Cone Degeneration (Optigen DNA-based test results registered with the OFA)
• Elbow Dysplasia (optional: OFA evaluation)
• Autoimmune Thyroiditis (optional: OFA evaluation from an approved laboratory; test repeated every three years)

For more information on these diseases, and others that affect the GSP, see Chapter 6: "Health and Nutrition."

Tell It Like It Is. Reputable breeders don't sugarcoat the breed. They want you to have a GSP that fits your expectations, and they want your expectations to fit your new GSP. When these two worlds meet, it is nirvana.

Ask Questions. The high-quality breeder will want to know a lot about you, your lifestyle, your experience with dogs, your commitment to training and exercise, and your expectations for a GSP in the home. By asking a lot of questions about you and your GSP goals, the breeder can make a better fit between you and a puppy.

Require Responsible Ownership. Show-potential puppies will be sold with a show contract, requiring you to show the dog unless the dog does

HOME BASICS
Safe Internet Surfing for a High-Quality Breeder

The Internet can be an amazing source of information, but as with anything else, much of the information is flawed, erroneous, or just flat-out wrong. The same is true when searching the Internet for a high-quality breeder. Today the Internet is flooded with puppy mills and brokers posing as "good" breeders who make it easy to "order" that hard-to-find breed at a great price.

Fortunately, an increasing number of high-quality breeders have developed web sites to record their dogs' accomplishments, announce upcoming litters, and, most important, share their experiences with the breed and provide honest, valuable information that benefits all GSP owners.

Problem is, it's hard to tell the high-quality breeders from the not-so-reputable breeders. The not-so-reputable breeders often have very slick, professional-looking web sites and appear to say all the right things. Even their photos are of beautiful dogs. Beware: Even the photos may not be what they seem. Breeders across the country have found photos "lifted" from their web sites and placed on other so-called breeders' pages!

The following are some red flags that can help you determine if you are looking at a less-than-reputable breeder's web site (and if so, should move on to another site):

✗ Accepts all major credit cards or PayPal as payment
✗ Will ship anywhere
✗ Ships puppies younger than eight weeks old
✗ Does not require any direct contact with you or ask for any references (if the puppy would need to be shipped)
✗ Does not answer phone calls and corresponds only by e-mail
✗ Does not allow you to come to the home to pick up the puppy
✗ Lists dogs with pet names and will not provide registered names (which are needed to search health records)
✗ Registers the puppies with an obscure kennel club
✗ Produces multiple litters a year but is selling all puppies (and not keeping any to show, trial, or otherwise compete)
✗ Breeds dogs that are younger than a year old and/or breeds every heat cycle
✗ Badmouths show breeders or field-trial breeders and does not personally show or compete in field events
✗ Is not a member of any national, regional, or local breed or hunt clubs
✗ Swears the GSP is as healthy as a horse and doesn't have any health problems, which is why he or she doesn't perform any health tests

not grow up to its potential (as determined by the breeder) and may require co-ownership, breeding rights, or other restrictions. Field-potential puppies will be sold with similar restrictions. Pet-quality puppies generally will be sold with a limited registration, requiring proof of spaying/neutering by a certain age before the breeder transfers the pup's registration to full-registration status.

Will Be a Mentor for Life. The high-quality breeder's love for the GSP is boundless, and the breeder's desire to share all things GSP with you is virtually limitless. This person is a wealth of information, and regardless of the breeder's "fame and glory" in the world of GSPs, he or she should make you feel as if there is no dog question that is too silly to ask.

Finding a High-Quality Breeder

So, you know the qualities of an experienced, responsible GSP breeder, but how do you find these people? It's easy, if you know where to look.

Breeder Referral

National sources, such as the GSPCA and the North American Versatile Hunting Dog Association (NAVHDA), regional GSP breed clubs, and local gundog clubs and all-breed clubs maintain a list of breeders who are members in good standing and often are required to abide by certain rules to be listed. To find breeder listings for the GSPCA or NAVHDA, see "Resources" for web site information. On the GSPCA's web site, you will also be able to find regional GSP breed clubs listed by state. Local all-breed clubs are listed with the AKC, and local gundog clubs are often sanctioned clubs of a national hunt club (see "Resources" for additional contact information).

Keep in mind that when you contact a breeder from a referral list, he or she may or may not have puppies available. Often, breeders may have as litters as infrequently as every other year or they may have one or two litters in a year. It depends on what the goals of the breeders are and if they are training, handling, and competing themselves or if the dogs are being sent to professional trainers and handlers for competition.

Regardless, after the breeder talks to you about what you are looking for and your interests, he or she may suggest you wait for an upcoming litter or refer you to someone he or she knows personally who may have a puppy that would suit your needs perfectly. You may wind up talking to two or three breeders before you find someone who may be a suitable match with an upcoming litter—or a litter already on the ground.

Dog Shows

Finding a dog show in your area is easy: go to *www.akc.org* or *www.infodog. com/showcalendar* for a listing of dog shows by state and date. A week before the show, the ring times and entries will be posted online, making it even easier to figure out when to attend the show to see the GSPs. While at the show, purchase a show catalog so that you have a way to contact the owners of dogs that are being exhibited at the show. Keep in mind that some owners handle their own dogs (talk to them after the judging is over!), whereas other owners have professional handlers show their dogs. Though the handler is not the dog's owner, he or she will be able to give you a way to contact the dog's breeder or owner. In either case, don't wait until the dog is about to enter the ring; approach them beforehand and ask if it's a good time to talk or if you can talk after they're finished showing that dog.

Field Trials, Hunt Tests, and More

See "Resources" for a listing of organizations that hold hunting tests and trials (and Chapter 10: "For German Shorthairs Especially" for a detailed description of the type of events each hunting organization holds). Go to the organizations' web sites to check for a schedule of upcoming tests and trials. Though AKC field trials can be a bit intense and are very competitive, those who are not actively competing and are in the gallery watching the trial will usually be happy to talk with newcomers to the sport. Hunt tests, however, reign supreme in friendliness and camaraderie, as these events are not competitive and though exceptionally challenging, tend to have more the air of a pleasant, family sporting event. Here you will find scores of people to talk to about the GSP and will easily meet breeders and owners who range from novices to experienced trainers.

Choosing a GSP Puppy

You've found a great breeder and now you're at the breeder's home, looking at a litter of eight happy, energetic puppies. Males, females, and everyone looks a bit different. How do you decide?

First of all, you may not have all eight puppies from which to choose. A high-quality breeder will have selected his or her "pick." (This is why the breeder bred this litter—to improve the breed and produce perhaps the next show or field champion.) A popular breeding, or one that has the potential to produce many show or hunting prospects, may have reservations placed for several more puppies. You yourself may have made a deposit on a puppy that hadn't been born yet! The breeder will most likely have some ideas about which puppy, of those available, might best suit your interests and expectations for a companion dog.

Even with the breeder's insights, you might still have to make a choice between several puppies. If this is the case, here are a few guidelines to help you make your selection.

Visit the puppies more than once. Realistically, this may not be possible. You may have flown or driven many hours and the day you meet the puppies is the day you need to make a selection. If you have the opportunity, however, to visit the puppies several times (and at different times of the day), you'll get a better idea of their emerging temperaments, drives, and activity levels. Sleepy puppies that

Breed Truths

A dominant personality is not necessarily bad, as often the very boldest puppies excel in competition. If you choose a pushy pup, be prepared to make sure you have the leadership abilities to maintain a balanced relationship with your dog.

PERSONALITY POINTERS
Puppy Aptitude Testing

The world of behaviorists is divided when it comes to how to test a puppy's aptitude and how valuable these tests are. For the most part, it is agreed that there isn't one particular test that is terribly accurate, as genetics and environment both play a role in whether a puppy reaches his genetic potential.

Test	How You Test
Boldness	Place an open cardboard box on the floor near the puppies.
Trust	Gently interlock fingers under a puppy's belly and just barely lift him from the floor; his paws should not be more than a quarter inch from the floor.
Reactivity	Stand a couple of yards away from the puppies and smack two blocks of wood together to make a loud noise.
Field potential	Tie some pigeon feathers to the end of a fishing line and "wiggle" it.
Companion potential	Call the pup over to you while sitting on the floor.

have just eaten a big meal may appear to be calm and quiet. Compare this with puppies that have just woken up from a nap and are furiously running, tumbling, gnawing, and barking. If you're able to see the pups multiple times, you'll be able to get a better idea for how the pups act overall.

Watch the puppies interact. It's a lot like watching kids on the playground: Some play nicely, some are bullies, and some don't want to play with anyone. The puppy that plays nicely is often a good choice. Don't overlook, however, the puppy that learns from his mistakes. In other words, if a puppy is offensive (makes another puppy yelp), it's okay if he recognizes his mistake and plays gently. It's not okay if he doesn't get the message and bullies the other puppy.

Who likes you? When you call, "Puppy, puppy, puppy!" is there a puppy that comes running to you to see what's going on? When you walk away quietly from the pack of puppies, is there a puppy that walks out of the pack to see what you are doing? Is there a particular puppy that is insistent on getting your attention? If a puppy meets your criteria and the puppy picks you, do not discount this one. Many, many longtime dog own-

The following tests can be helpful in determining where a puppy is at the moment of testing. (Time spent with the puppy's parents is probably a better indicator of how the puppy might develop as an adult if he is given an optimum environment.)

What You're Looking For

A puppy that shows curiosity without timidity (tail down, crouching toward the box). Barking at the box is okay if it is playful and curious and not fear barking.

A puppy that is relatively relaxed and doesn't immediately bark and growl, wriggle hard, or bite to be put back down.

Expect the puppies to jump when they hear the blocks, but watch to see how the puppies react afterward. You want to see the puppies look toward the noise with curiosity. Indifference is also okay, but the puppy that has been obviously frightened by the noise may be a little sensitive, overreactive, or fearful.

Some puppies will point, but they should at least show a keen interest in it and "want" it.

Lots of excited puppy kisses, and sometimes the launching of a puppy body into your arms!

ers, trainers, and breeders will swear that if you are lucky enough to have a puppy (or adult dog) pick you as his special person, you cannot go wrong.

Is the moderate puppy best? Ages ago, the sage puppy-buying advice was to steer clear of the dominant puppy in the litter, avoid the quietest puppy, and choose one of the "pups in the middle." The thought here was that in order to avoid picking a puppy that could grow up to be an overly dominant or aggressive dog or an excessively fearful puppy, you should avoid the "extremes" of the litter. The only problem with this thinking is that it is quite possible that, for example, an entire litter of pups has exceptional drive and boldness. If you are seeking a field-trial dog, you want that drive and boldness, so you might want the boldest, pushiest pup of the lot because you know what you want and you're experienced with field dogs. If you're seeking a companion, however, it would be a mistake to avoid the calmest pup of the litter, because that might be the perfect puppy for you! If you are working with an experienced breeder, he or she will be able to help guide you to the puppy or puppies that have the potential to most closely meet your expectations.

Look for good health. If you're working with a reputable breeder, the puppies should be the image of health. Their coats should be smooth and free of dirt and debris. Their eyes should be clear, bright, and clear of discharge. There should be no signs of intestinal distress, and though fat, round tummies look cute, overly fat, round tummies could be a sign of intestinal parasites. Also, look to see the condition of the pups' mother; she should be clean and have the appearance of good health, too.

Rescues, Shelters, and Other Facilities Compared

Depending on where you adopt your GSP, you may find that the shelter provides everything from complete veterinary workups to temperament testing and "basic training," or you may be left pretty much on your own when selecting and evaluating a dog.

The following are some of the most commonly seen differences between organizations that offer dogs for adoption:

National GSP Rescue

The National GSP Rescue organization is an affiliate of the GSPCA and is the "parent" organization for regional and local GSP rescue groups. Start with their web site (*www.rescue.gspca.org*) to find a rescue group close to you.

Typically, breed-specific rescues are of the highest quality and are run by people who live, breathe, and love the breed. GSP rescues are no exception. Though services may vary from rescue to rescue, generally all dogs offered for adoption have had a complete veterinary exam, and are spayed or neutered, temperament tested, crate trained (content to rest in a crate when asked), housetrained (or in the process of being housetrained), know a few basic commands, and have been evaluated for their acceptance of other dogs and small children. Since GSP rescues are particularly cognizant of the GPS tendency to be "sharp" toward cats, most rescues try to determine if the GSP is aggressive toward cats; however, this is not possible to determine in some situations. GSPs in the breed-rescue network are kept in foster homes while receiving medical care and being evaluated. Prospective adopters will meet available GSPs in home settings, giving adopters a good idea about how the dog behaves in the home.

Nonprofit Shelters

The level of services and the quality of the shelter facility depend largely on the charity of those living in the surrounding community. When money is exceptionally tight, most organizations try to do the best they can with what they have, but their services may be very limited. Well-funded organizations simply can afford to offer more services, and numerous nonprofit shelters are offering such benefits as on-staff animal behaviorists, reduced-rate veterinary services, year-round training classes, and more.

Except in special cases in which a dog may leave the shelter to live in a foster home, most dogs in a shelter are kept in kennels. Shelter staff do make an effort to determine how a dog might adapt to home life and evaluate how the dog reacts to other dogs and cats.

Municipally Run "Pounds" or Animal Control

Depending on the city and the importance it places on its shelter, the facility could be a dismal, barebones place that holds strays until their "time" runs out and they are euthanized. Other cities have made a real investment in their shelters and provide the same services as some of the top nonprofit shelters. Adopting a GSP from a municipally run shelter, therefore, could run the gamut of experiences.

The Adoption Process

To adopt a GSP from a local pound or animal control center, the application process is usually fairly simple. You will need to be 21 years old and able to show proof of residence. Fees are minimal, with $40 to $60 being fairly standard; however, as these facilities improve their services, the adoption fee

BE PREPARED! Top Ten Benefits of Adopting an Adult

Reason 10: The Edge Is Off. The first three or four years of owning a GSP can be challenging to those who aren't used to owning a high-energy dog. An older adult GSP, particularly one that is seven or eight, will be more sedate than a younger dog and may be just what you are looking for!

Reason 9: Health Problems Are Identified. By the time a dog has reached adulthood, many chronic and/or potentially serious hereditary illnesses can be diagnosed. Additionally, if an adult dog has an illness or condition, you will know what the cost of his treatment will be and any limitations he might have.

Reason 8: Temperament Is Formed. You won't have to worry about how the temperament of an adult dog will be when he grows up, because he is grown up. If the rescued GSP has formed a terrific temperament despite neglect, an enriched, loving, solid home will help him truly blossom.

Reason 7: What You See Is Really What You Get. With puppies, there's always that edge of uncertainty about how big or lean or long the dog will get as he matures. With an adult dog, there are no surprises.

Reason 6: Housetraining Is a Snap. A young puppy may need to relieve himself every two to four hours, depending on his activity level. An adult dog, if on an eating/drinking/exercise schedule, can hold it up to six hours during the day and can easily sleep through the night. This makes housetraining much easier.

Reason 5: Routine Veterinary Care Is Complete. Most GSP rescues and shelters fully vaccinate dogs before adoption, and if spaying/neutering isn't included in the adoption fee, it is usually offered at a reduced rate.

Reason 4: Bargain Priced. Rescued GSPs cost a fraction of the cost of a puppy, and are just as loving. And they may cost you less in other ways, too. (See Reason 3!)

Reason 3: Less Destruction. Most older adult dogs are beyond the heavy chewing, shredding, and nipping stage. Be forewarned, however, that this breed typically doesn't completely outgrow their destructive phase until they are at least three or four years of age. If the dog you are adopting is younger, he may be at a shelter because of his chewing. He will still outgrow it, eventually, but you need to be prepared for this possibility.

Reason 2: Ready, Set, Go! If you purchase a puppy, before you can really start socializing him, you will have to wait until he is far enough along in his vaccination series that your veterinarian gives you the okay to take him into the world. On the other hand, if you adopt an adult GSP, he is ready to play with other dogs, go on walks through popular parks, and take training classes the moment you bring him home.

Reason 1: When Was the Last Time Someone Picked You to Idolize? Perhaps the greatest advantage to adopting an adult dog is that the process allows the dog to tell you he wants you as his owner. When there's mutual adoration and love, it's always a win-win situation.

FYI: Adopting an Adult GSP

If you're considering adopting an adult GSP, the good news is that you will be able to choose from quite a few dogs. The bad news, of course, is that there are too many GSPs that find their way into shelters and rescues. And, of course, they will all want to come home with you. As a potential adopter, it is important to select the right dog for your situation.

may go higher as will the adoption requirements (with well-funded facilities requiring the same application process as below).

At a nonprofit shelter, in addition to meeting the age and residency requirements, you will be asked to fill out a questionnaire and most likely a staff member will give you an informal interview (it could be so informal, you may think it's casual conversation). If the shelter has any GSPs in the facility, you will get to meet them. If you find a dog you're interested in, the rest of your family members will get to meet the dog. If you have one or more dogs at home, you'll be asked to bring your current dog to the shelter, where a staff member will oversee the initial introduction (on "neutral" territory) to the potential new dog.

If you're adopting from a GSP rescue in the National GSP Rescue network, you will go through all the steps listed above, and depending on the individual rescue with which you're working, it is likely that the rescue will want someone to come to your home and do a "home check" before you're allowed to adopt a GSP. If the adopter has any issues in the home or yard that could be potentially challenging with a GSP, the experienced rescue volunteer can help the individual by giving him or her suggestions or solutions.

What to Expect

Rescued GSPs are wonderful, and perhaps what makes the bond a bit magical is that when adopting a dog through breed rescue, the dog is allowed to "pick" his forever home. Those who have worked in rescue or who have experienced the moment a dog "picks" you will testify that it's a done deal. There is no greater match than one in which you have been selected. It is important, however, not to assume that this is the moment that the violins start to play and everything becomes perfect for the life of the dog. This is a dog. He will need to adapt to his new home and family. Take things slowly with a rescued GSP. Work to build a solid bond between you and dog. Earn his trust and he will earn yours. (It also helps to have patience and a sense of humor.)

Once you've formed a bond with your GSP (and this could take days, weeks, or even months, depending on the dog), you will have a companion for life … a companion that will truly give you his heart.

Chapter Four

Caring for a New German Shorthaired Pointer

You are about to bring your new puppy (or rescued adult dog) home and spend the day playing and showering your dog with love and affection, but is everything at home ready? Being prepared for your new shorthair's arrival at home can save you from a lot of problems later (and last-minute trips to the pet store to quickly purchase what you needed).

Preparing for Your GSP's Arrival

The first thing you want to do is to make your home and yard "GSP-safe"—which can be even more difficult than making something "child-safe." Remember, your shorthair is a gundog with an incredible nose and an ever-working mind. He will find things to explore and chew that you would not have imagined would even be attractive to a dog. Your job, as a new GSP owner, is to figure out what your puppy could possibly get into and make sure he can't get into it.

Indoors
The most dangerous areas indoors are typically the kitchen and bathrooms, where poisonous and caustic cleaning materials are often kept under the sink behind floor-height cabinet doors. Invest in kid-cabinet locks that prevent the easy opening of cabinets. (Also, consider kid-drawer locks, because GSPs are quite adept at pulling open drawers if they think there's something good in them.)

Be very careful, too, about where you keep medications. Chewing on pill containers seems to be a hobby of some dogs, but ingesting the contents could be fatal. Keep all prescription—and nonprescription—containers out of reach and behind closed cabinets. This list should include NSAIDs, vitamins, and supplements.

Garbage and trash cans should be behind locked cabinet doors, and taken out nightly. A heavy, well-made, stainless-steel, tight-lidded garbage can may be okay to have out in the kitchen while the shorthair is supervised, but this container is not safe while the puppy or dog is left unattended. The GSP will get into the garbage, strew the contents across the kitchen floor, and eat the best parts. You can try to spend countless hours to train your dog not to raid the garbage can, but it's much easier to lock it up out of sight.

Many people now have home offices, and with the home office comes a myriad of electrical cords. Puppies (and some adults) find these cords irresistible chew items. Keep the cords grouped together, and use cord covers (sold

Poisonous Plants

There is a long list of common house-plants and outdoor, garden plants that are poisonous to dogs. Amaryllis, crocus, aza-leas, lilies, begonias, certain types of ivy, carnations, birds of paradise, the stems, leaves, and seeds of cherries, cyclamens, daisies, and elephant ears—the list goes on and on. If you have any of these plants in your home or in your yard, keep your shorthair from having access to them.

A complete list of poisonous plants is available through the ASPCA and can be accessed online at *www.aspca.org/Pet-care/poison-control/Plants*. If you cannot reach your veterinarian for assistance, the ASPCA maintains a 24-hour emergency poison hotline that can be accessed for questions (and a consultation fee) at (888) 426-4435. It is a good idea to keep this number handy in a central location or your cell phone for emergency questions.

by office-supply retailers and online) to keep them safely secured to the floor or wall and out of harm's way. Additionally, make sure that paper clips, jammed staples, and other metal objects are thrown away completely and not tossed in the office trash can if the can is easily accessible to the puppy.

Are you a trinket-on-the-coffee-table kind of person? This would be a good time to put those items up and into cabi-nets for viewing. Even if your shorthair doesn't have a penchant for eating small figurines, he will often have periods of boisterousness that will knock over any item that is not firmly secured.

Outdoors

When examining your backyard for potential puppy or adult dangers, be sure to know what types of plants are in your yard and know, too, if they are poisonous. (See "Helpful Hint: Poisonous Plants.") Highly poisonous plants should be relocated from the yard or blocked off with fencing.

Check your wood fencing for loose boards, rotten areas, exposed nails, and other areas that could make the fence unsafe for your puppy or provide an easy escape route for a curious dog. If you have a chain-link fence, make sure it is sunk below ground level to prevent digging out and is tall enough (at least 6 feet [1.8 m]) to prevent your dog from climbing over.

Examine your wood decks and crawl spaces, because these are really cool (literally) places for a puppy or adult dog to explore. He may become stuck and/or injured and unable to get out. Block off access to all these areas with strong lattice or garden fencing.

Breed Needs

Shorthairs should never be let loose in the yard unsupervised, because they are sure to find a way out. If you have a fence climber or digger-under who is adept at escaping even if left in the yard for brief periods of time (i.e., you go back inside to grab the phone and come out and your shorthair is gone), it may be necessary to add an electric fence and train your shorthair on it. Note that an electric fence alone is never a good idea for a shorthair who has the determination and drive to bull his way through the fence. He may suffer the shock but then be unwilling to come back into the yard.

If you own a pool, you will need to take additional precautions to keep your GSP safe. If your pool doesn't have additional fencing around it, never allow your shorthair in the yard without your supervision and the ability to retrieve him from the pool safely. Teach him at an early age to use the steps to get out of the pool; shorthairs love water and are excellent swimmers, but unless they know where the steps to the pool are, they can't possibly get out and will drown. When pool season is over, invest in a pool cover that is rated as a safety cover and will support the adult shorthair's weight if he walks out onto it.

The First Day

There is nothing more exciting than the first day your GSP is home with you. You won't be able to resist spending every second you can with him, even if it is letting him snuggle in your lap while sleeping blissfully.

Keep Things Calm

Resist the temptation to have a "puppy party" the first day—or even week—that your shorthair is home. The first few days with your puppy should be time for him to bond with you and your family. Though he will have been raised in a home, the sights and sounds of your home will be different from those of the breeder's, and this is his time to comfortably acclimate himself to his new surroundings and get on a schedule. Allow him time to investigate where everything is. It won't take him long to remember where his water bowl is. It will definitely not take him long to know where he is to be fed! Once he's gotten comfortable and completely at ease in your home, it is fine to invite over a few people at a time to meet him.

Watch for any signs of stress, especially if there is a large crowd of people there to "greet" him. (See "The Art of Socialization" for more tips on signs of stress and making positive introductions to people.)

Provide Supervision
Your shorthair won't come housetrained, so keep an eye on him (see "Housetraining," page 64). Also, watch what he is doing. Is he tugging on the lamp cord? Chewing on the rug's tassels? Gnawing on the kitchen-table legs? Remove him from areas where he could damage (or be damaged). When he's little, an exercise pen (or two attached to make a bigger play area) can be very handy.

Make It a Routine
Puppies respond well to a regular routine, and it helps them acclimate to their new home a little more quickly. Start now by establishing when you feed him (two to three meals a day), when you exercise him, and when he is expected to snuggle in for the night.

Don't Push Too Hard
Yes, this is a breed that is known for its endurance. However, as a puppy, you will find that your shorthair needs a lot of sleep. He will play hard and sleep hard. Make sure he gets his puppy sleep, and don't take him on long walks (i.e., miles and miles …) until he's a little older.

Puppy's First Night

Puppies are going to cry that first night (and sometimes a few more), if alone in their bed or crate. They are away from home for the first time and no longer have the comfort, warmth, and safety of their mother and litter-mates. GSPs are extremely intelligent, and being "alone" will "hit them" the most when they are physically alone.

Keep him company. Put his crate near or next to your bed. Knowing he is not alone can help, although he will definitely try to persuade you to let him sleep snuggled next to you in bed. (This is fine if you want him to sleep with you, but it isn't wise to allow a puppy to sleep in your bed until he is able to sleep through the night. Otherwise, you may wake to find a present in your bed.)

Keep him warm. Think about it. He's used to sleeping in a warm puppy pile, and now he's all alone and very possibly cold. Make sure his crate is in a comfortable place without any drafts. If you've chosen a wire crate for him, consider adding a crate cover or wrapping a heavy blanket around his crate. Do be sure that he's not able to tug the blanket into his crate and eat it. For bedding in the crate, you can provide a thick layer of newspaper and make it even deeper and warmer by adding shredded newspaper.

Keep him busy. Much like a baby might take a pacifier when he/she is sleepy, giving a shorthair a "busy" chew to work on when it's bedtime can help him adjust to his night alone.

Make it familiar. DAP is an artificial form of the hormone produced by a lactating female dog. Your puppy will find this scent soothing and famil-iar. DAP can be sprayed lightly on the pup's bedding or used as an atomizer in the crate or room.

Be aware of his needs. He may not be kidding—he may need to relieve himself! You will quickly learn the differ-ence in his night sounds when he really, truly

SHOPPING LIST

Puppy's Safe Toys and Chews List

✔ GSPs have a talent for being able to destroy the indestructible. Most toys are only as safe as the supervision you provide. Generally speaking, don't leave any soft, fluffy toys with your GSP unattended. If there's a way to shred it, he will find it.

✔ The best choices for toys are those built and designed for "heavy" chewers. Avoid hard shinbones, as these can break a puppy or adult's teeth. A great toy is a heavy, stuffable Kong that provides the pup with at least 30 minutes of activity time trying to lick and chew the cheesy or peanut-buttery treat out of it.

✔ Chews range in safety, too. Bones made of rawhide soften as the dogs chew. In a softened state, they can be bitten off in large chunks and either swallowed (possibly causing a deadly intestinal obstruction) or choked on.

needs to relieve himself. Be sure to give him an opportunity to relieve himself every few hours that first night, no matter how tired you might be.

And a warning: The drive and determination that makes the GSP such a remarkable hunting dog can make him a bit stubborn and equally determined to outlast you at night until you get him out of his crate. If you are positive that he's not cold and that he doesn't have to relieve himself, you have to be more determined than he is!

BE PREPARED! German Shorthaired Pointer Supplies

Before your shorthair comes home, make a checklist of items you will need. The following are the basics that you should have on hand for your shorthair's arrival.

Food: What kind of food does your GSP's breeder recommend? If you can, buy the identical brand and transition to another brand later, if you feel you need to. (GSPs are not nearly as "sensitive" to food transitions as some breeds, so don't agonize over this.)

Bowls: Purchase bowls for both food and water. Try to get weighted bowls that won't tip over when your puppy inevitably steps on them and in them. You will always want fresh water available, so you will want at least two bowls. (Note that there is nothing wrong with using bowls you already have, but if they are plastic, they will be chewed to pieces.)

Crate: You will definitely want a crate. Crate training and the ability to crate a GSP are essential for your mental health. Your GSP should not be too cramped in his crate. He will need to be able to stand up, turn around, and lie down comfortably. If you purchase a crate specifically to fit your puppy, be aware that you will need to purchase additional crates as your puppy grows—unless you purchase a full-size crate that has a movable puppy barrier. The movable puppy barrier allows you to adjust the amount of living space within the crate.

Tip: An easy and inexpensive way to make a full-size crate suitable for a puppy is to place a cardboard box in the crate to make his living area smaller. Make sure the box does not have any staples, which would be dangerous for the puppy to ingest (as the puppy will likely chew on the box).

Both plastic and sturdy wire crates are excellent choices for the shorthair puppy; however, try to make sure that the grate size of the wire crate is small enough that a puppy mouth can't chew on the wire.

Bedding: Something soft, but not too fluffy and shreddable/edible, is preferred. GSPs, particularly bored puppies, will shred and ingest bedding, with disastrous results. Until your puppy is older (and you've got your exercise, play, and training routine down) you may want to line your pup's crate with a layer of newspapers or pee pads.

Collar: GSPs don't usually have a problem with neck hair being "rubbed off" by a collar. You can use a basic, plain buckle collar or a flat, quick-snap collar. (Do not use a training collar, as they can easily get caught on something and strangle your puppy.) Make sure your collar has a ring for attaching ID and rabies tags as well as a leash for walks. Check the collar often as your puppy grows and adjust the size accordingly. The collar should be snug but allow for two fingers to be slipped between the collar and the pup's neck.

Identification Tag: Before you bring your puppy home, be sure to have an ID tag made up with the pup's name and your cell phone number with area code—not your home phone. If you are traveling, you will have your cell phone with you. If you are out looking for your lost GSP, you will have your cell phone on you. If someone finds your lost pup and calls your home phone, you won't be home! Eventually, you will want to have your shorthair microchipped for permanent identification (see "Identification Options, page 63).

Leash: Keep your leashes out of "chew" range. They can be nylon or leather. A good length to have is the basic 6-foot (1.8 m) leash. Consider buying a lighter-weight leash with a smaller buckle for a young puppy. There's nothing worse than having a heavy brass clip clunk the pup in the side of the head. It doesn't provide a very good experience.

Stain and Odor Removers: It's not a matter of if but when your shorthair has an accident. Be prepared! Many of today's products have no perfumes and work by having enzymes or microbes break down or "eat" the unseen residue. These are much safer for your puppy than those with surfactants or dangerous chemicals.

Anti-Chew Salve and Sprays: Though the best way to keep a puppy from chewing on something he's not supposed to is (1) give him an appropriate and yummy chew, and (2) keep him away from inappropriate items, there will be certain things in your home that your shorthair may become fixated on chewing. Though GSPs are renowned for their nonaversion to things that taste horrible or bitter, it's always worth a try to use an anti-chew salve or spray to keep the pup away from table legs, cabinet doors, windowsills, and so on.

Dog Appeasing Pheromone (DAP): This synthetic pheromone mimics the scent of a hormone produced by lactating female dogs. Both puppies and adults find this scent comforting. The product can be used as a spray on the pet's bedding or as an atomizer on the pup's crate or the room where he'll be trying to rest.

Exercise Pen: An exercise pen or ex-pen is a terrific way to keep a little puppy out of trouble while you're at home but can't keep your full attention on him.

Dog Gates: Plan which rooms in the home you want to keep your shorthair out of or in, and use sturdy metal dog gates to keep the room secured. Wooden, temporary gates are fine for small puppies, but a more determined, older shorthair will need the type of gate that actually fastens into studs in your walls.

Pee Pads: Newspapers are fine to line a crate or ex-pen with; however, they are not waterproof. Pee pads are more expensive, but they are also very absorbent and provide a waterproof barrier from the floor.

Preventing Separation Anxiety

GSPs are bred to work with their owners, so they form a very close bond to them. Many do not like being separated from their owners, but this can vary widely from dog to dog. A lot of cases of "separation anxiety" aren't actually separation anxiety at all. It's simply a bored, restless dog with an opportunity to destroy something.

What Is Separation Anxiety?

True separation anxiety (SA) is an extremely stressful reaction to the owner leaving. There are varying levels of SA—from mild (a lot of drooling, whining, barking, pacing, panting, and continued restlessness until the owner returns) to extreme (the dog is so panicked that he can't be crated because he will bloody himself trying to claw his way out of the crate, urination, defecation, mass destruction of furniture, blinds, doors, and anything else that might separate him from his owner). The key is that with SA, the dog never relaxes and the stressful behaviors persist the entire time you are away.

Breed Truths

If you aren't sure if your shorthair has SA or needs more exercise and mental stimulation, set up a video or audio recorder (or a live feed from your computer's webcam) and listen to and watch what he does. If the symptoms disappear shortly after you're gone, he doesn't have SA. If he is relaxed and then goes and tears something up, he doesn't have SA. He has SA only if his stressful behaviors persist for the duration of your absence.

FYI: Your Rescued Adult GSP's First Days

A rescued adult GSP may already be crate-trained and housetrained, but don't assume this to be the case. As a rescue dog, depending on the treatment he received and the experiences he had with his prior owner, he may be more "wary" of his new surroundings, or being in a home may be completely unfamiliar.

As with a puppy, make his introduction into the new home a calm and quiet one. Do not invite a ton of people over to meet your new dog until he has bonded closely with you and your family and is completely acclimated to your home. This may be a matter of days, or it could be a week or longer.

Be patient, and spend time with him. Begin his crate training, make sure he has lots of exercise and walks, and start on some basic obedience training (see Chapter 7 "Training and Activities"). It is advisable to ensure that the rescue dog sleeps comfortably in his crate and understands his position as "follower" (with you as the "leader") in the family before allowing him a spot on the bed, if that is what you want eventually.

Additionally, be keenly aware of any signs of stress and know how to prevent stress in your adopted GSP (see "GSP Body Language").

Most shorthairs adapt quickly to their new homes; just be sure to take it slowly with your new adult dog.

SA is triggered by "leaving" behaviors. A shorthair with SA knows your entire routine from locking the back door and grabbing your computer bag to picking up the front keys off the hall table. Treating SA involves several different approaches, including a desensitization program to your "leaving" cues as well as anti-anxiety medication in addition to a desensitization program.

One of the best ways to prevent SA is to acclimate your new shorthair to your leaving. Often, people purchase a puppy and bring him home during a short holiday or a long vacation (i.e., summer break). The puppy is used to people being with him 24/7 and taking him everywhere.

These are all good things; however, when the kids go back to school in the fall or the winter holidays are over, the puppy is suddenly alone. The owners have done nothing to prepare the pup for this, and because he is a close-working gundog that thrives on human attention, this sudden withdrawal can cause the onset of SA.

Five Preventive Steps

To prepare your shorthair for periods of aloneness (without suffering anxiety from the separation) there are several steps you can take.

1. Acclimate him to his crate. The shorthair's crate should be a place of comfort and refuge. Don't suddenly spring the idea of a crate on the day you're leaving him.

FYI: A Resource for Separation Anxiety

One of the best resources (besides your veterinarian) is the booklet by Patricia McConnell, PhD, *I'll Be Home Soon: How to Prevent and Treat Separation Anxiety* (McConnell Publishing, June 1, 2000). The 38-page booklet contains a six-week training plan for severe separation anxiety, as well as solid tips for treating mild and moderate cases.

2. Practice leaving him, but leave him occupied. Carve out little bits of time where you walk out of the room while he's playing in his ex-pen or gnawing on a great chew toy. Five or ten minutes is good. Then return and reward him if he's been quiet. If he's been noisy or fussy, don't make a big deal over it, and reward him once he's quieted down again.
3. Leave him alone for longer times. With him well pottied and occupied with a good chew toy, leave the house for 30 minutes to an hour.
4. Exercise him well before leaving him. A tired pup is more likely to associate his crate with relaxing. Your leaving will be less stressful, because there's no more pent-up energy.

5. Don't make a fuss over him. It's hard not to make a big fuss over a puppy that is so overjoyed to see that you've come back, but resist. Be matter-of-fact as you leave and return. Maintain an air of confidence so your shorthair doesn't become anxious with you leaving.

If you've done your preventive training well, your GSP is old enough to be fully housetrained, and you feel your GSP is ready for staying "loose" in the home when you are away, begin with short periods of time, and gradually increase the time away. Observe how he does. Some GSPs do very, very well alone. Others never do well enough not to use a crate while their humans are gone. You will have to determine what your GSP needs.

Acclimating to the Crate

It is not cruel to crate-train a dog. Do not let your GSP convince you otherwise, unless you enjoy coming home to a swath of destruction in your home. GSPs adapt quickly to a crate, as long as they know you are not willing to negotiate. To make it a little easier on your GSP, particularly with an adopted adult shorthair that may not have had a lot of crate time or had a negative experience, you can do the following.

Keep him close by. Keep the crate in an area where your GSP can watch what's going on. He will not feel so lonely and isolated. This may mean you'll need more than one crate in the home (for example, one in the

---

BE PREPARED! Different Crates for Different GSPs

Crates come in essentially two kinds: collapsible wire and a combination of hard plastic and wire mesh (the typical shipping crate used by airlines, like VariKennel). Either crate will work just fine for a GSP. Often, those who go to dog shows prefer the wire crates, because they stack better in a van and on top of each other. Wire crates have more ventilation (It's solid wire!), so they can be good particularly in the summer when a little extra air is appreciated. In the winter, you may need to purchase or make a crate wrap to keep out drafts. Also, make sure that when you're selecting a sturdy, solid wire crate, the wire mesh (which makes up the squares) is small enough that a puppy can't get his bottom jaw stuck on it.

Sometimes, dogs prefer being in more of a "lair" and prefer the hard plastic kind of crates. This crate typically comes in two pieces that fasten together with a metal mesh door and metal mesh panels on the side. Plastic crates get quite hot in the summer, and the addition of a battery-powered fan could be necessary when traveling in the car (the air-conditioning isn't going to make it into the crate very well). They do clean out very easily, so if there's an accident, it's simple to hose them out.

In the end, it is your choice, and you can train your GSP to adapt.

bedroom and one in the family room) or you may need to adjust to moving the crate during the day.

Feed him in his crate. GSPs love to eat. This will make being "in the crate" a good thing, at least at times. While he is eating, you can leave the crate door open.

Make it comfy. Unless your shorthair is a shredder, you can put something soft and snuggly in his crate to nestle in and nap on.

Use food rewards. Toss treats inside the crate to encourage your GSP to go into his kennel. Make everything positive for him about going into his crate. (A rescue dog may not have had prior positive experiences, so be patient.)

Don't forget DAP. The stuff really works for many dogs. It's worth a try.

Shut the door. Once your shorthair is comfortable going in and out of the crate, put him in and shut the door. (This is a good time to put in a chew or treat that takes a little while to eat.) Begin with short periods of time, and work your way up to longer periods.

When acclimating your GSP to his crate, be kind but persistent. If your GSP tells you that you are committing a grave injustice by "locking him up," ignore him and his Jedi mind tricks. In the end, you are doing something that could save his life and will help make him a better companion.

Identification Options

There are three different ways to identify your GSP should he get lost. Many owners choose to use at least two methods, whereas others use all three. There are drawbacks to each method; therefore, many owners try to cover all the angles.

Tags and ID Collar Plates

Tags and collar ID plates should always be used. No matter who finds your dog, he or she will almost assuredly first look for a dog tag or an ID plate affixed to the collar for owner information. Make sure your GSP's ID tag or plate is easy to read and has current information. Use your cell phone number, so if you are driving around trying to find your GSP or have lost him while you are out of town, you can receive a call on your cell phone. Also, regularly check the ring that attaches the tag to the collar. These often get loose and make it easier for a tag to fall off, which is the downside to using only collar identification. Basically, if the tag falls off or the plated collar is pulled off—or if the engraving on the plate or tag is so old, it's illegible— your shorthair has no way of being identified.

Tattoos

No, we're not talking about the "I love Mom" tattoo. This is a tattoo that is usually assigned a specific number from a registry and is tattooed on the inside of the dog's thigh. The shorthair does not have much hair here, so it is fairly legible if someone looks. The problem with tattoos is that often the average Good Samaritan doesn't think to look for one. Second, a tattoo does fade over time. And third, the dog needs to be under anesthesia to have the tattoo applied and should be of adult size so that the tattoo doesn't become illegible as the pup grows.

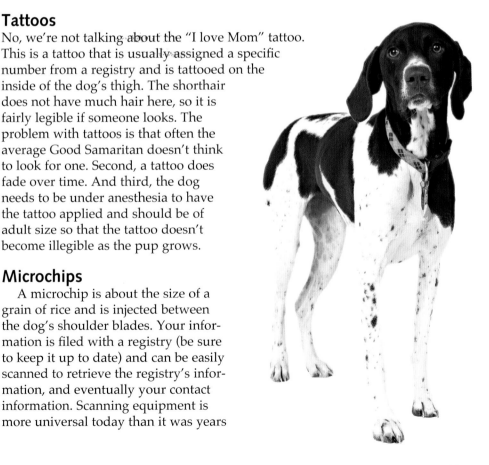

Microchips

A microchip is about the size of a grain of rice and is injected between the dog's shoulder blades. Your information is filed with a registry (be sure to keep it up to date) and can be easily scanned to retrieve the registry's information, and eventually your contact information. Scanning equipment is more universal today than it was years ago (when certain scanners were needed for certain chips). Veterinarians, shelters, and rescues are supposed to scan for these chips when a lost dog is presented to them. Rarely, a chip can fail or travel to a location beyond the shoulder blades. For the most part, however, this is one of the best ways—along with a collar ID tag or plate—to keep your dog identified.

Housetraining Made Easy

GSPs are usually relatively easy to train to be reliable in the home. As long as you don't give your shorthair too much space too soon, keep him on a regular eating and exercise schedule, and are aware of his physical limitations, the shorthair will housetrain quickly. Here are a few tips to get you started.

1. Dogs do not want to soil their "space." Even young puppies do not want to relieve themselves where they sleep or eat. Neither do adult dogs. If a dog is confined in an area too small for him to relieve himself in one spot and stay comfortably in another, he will "hold it" as long as he can until he is released from the area. The best training device you can use starting out is a comfortable crate.

2. Your dog's bladder is not infinite in capacity. Look at your young puppy and think about the actual size of his little bladder. It doesn't hold much, especially if the puppy is excited or running around. Your pup won't be able to "hold it" for more than two hours at a time (during awake hours) when he's little. By four months, he can probably

hold it for four hours and be better able to sleep through the night without an early morning break. A nervous or stressed adult may not be able to hold it much longer than a younger puppy at first because of the effect stress has on the manufacture (increased) of urine.

3. Know his schedule. Young puppies typically have to relieve themselves after the following: a round of hard play, awaking from a nap, a period of great excitement (you just came home!), coming out of the crate after a period of alone time, drinking a lot of water, and within a half hour of eating. Allow him plenty of time to relieve himself before crating him again or leaving him alone.

4. Don't be in a rush to give him more room. Remember, a crate is your friend. You don't have to increase the space your GSP is in when you're gone at any particular pace or schedule. Remember, it's not just housetraining that you must consider, but the likelihood of chewing and shredding in whatever space you give your GSP. Be patient! When you do start to give your GSP more room, do so gradually and keep a close eye on how he does. If he has an accident, examine whether you gave him too much room too quickly, Or, did you change his schedule in some way?

5. When your puppy is loose, keep a close eye on him at all times. Is he suddenly starting to sniff? Pick him up and take him outside. Is he beginning to circle? Pick him up and take him outside. Is he "sneaking" away, quietly, to another part of the house? Pick him up and take him outside. Don't wait, and don't move slowly. Puppies squat amazingly quickly.

6. Tell him he's good! You've picked him up and rushed outside, and your GSP puppy dutifully tinkles. This is a cause for calm celebration! Make him feel like he is the best puppy in the whole world.

What if he has an accident inside? Never, ever physically punish him. If he had an accident, it means that you missed something. You didn't allow him to relieve himself when he needed to or you gave him too much space too soon or he's a little guy and didn't know he had to go until he did.

The only time it is appropriate to say anything is if you catch him in the act. "In the act" is not the same as "walking away from" the act. It needs to be as your dog is lifting his leg or beginning to squat. If you catch him in the act, you can say, "Ah, ah, ah!" to stop the flow and then quickly (and gently—not angrily) carry or take him outside. When he finishes what he has to do, tell him how wonderful he is.

Then, clean up the mistake thoroughly—remember, these dogs have incredibly sensitive noses.

Perhaps most important, don't worry if a mistake is made. Ask yourself if you could have done anything better. For instance, did you let your puppy go too long from the last time he relieved himself? Did you ignore one of the warning signs that he had to go? Sometimes, accidents just happen, too. So don't lose your patience. Perseverance will win the day in the end.

If your adult shorthair who was previously housetrained begins having accidents in the home for no apparent reason, have him examined by your veterinarian. Urinary tract infections, incontinence, diabetes, canine cognitive dysfunction, and separation anxiety are just a few of the possible causes. If disease can be ruled out, then take a step back and reexamine the housetraining situation. Maybe you changed your dog's routine? Switched to a different food? Or maybe you became lax about your dog's schedule. Usually if there's no disease present, the housetraining issues can be resolved with a little patience and a little more control of the situation.

German Shorthaired Pointer Development

Stage: Neonatal (Birth to 2 weeks)
Liver roan markings start off looking more like white with ticking but darken over time. Within a day or two of birth, the GSP's tail is docked, either by his breeder or a veterinarian, to roughly 40 percent of its original length. (This may seem cruel, but without it being docked, a GSP would beat his tail to a bloody pulp from wagging in dense brush while hunting.) Eyes and ears are still closed.

Stage: Transitional (2–3 weeks)
The eyes open up at 2 weeks, although sight is not fully developed. The ear canals also open, and by 3 weeks of age, the shorthair puppy is hearing

very, very well. In these weeks he begins to grow rapidly and begins show-ing more coordination when moving around.

Stage: Socialization (3 to 12–13 weeks)
This is a time of great growth both physically and mentally for the shorthair puppy. The puppy learns to socialize in his interactions with his littermates, mother, and people. Having good experiences is critical; his environment is thought to make the most significant lasting impression on the pup during this time.

Additionally, milk teeth (those needle-sharp baby teeth) typically are in by 5 weeks, and this is when the mother finishes weaning her pups.

Stage: Adolescence (13 weeks to 11 months)
At 4 months, your GSP will show much better bladder control, and house-training will become much easier. At 5 months, your shorthair's adult teeth will have come in, and the weeks before, during, and after will be those of the heaviest, most destructive chewing by your shorthair. At 7 months, your GSP should reach his full height or be close to full height; however, he will still appear a bit gangly and immature. Sexual maturity will occur within the first 12 months, but can vary quite a bit from dog to dog. Male shorthairs that have not been neutered may begin marking territory in and outside the home at the age of 7 months.

Stage: Maturity (12 months to 2 years)
The shorthair will not grow in height, but he will continue to mature and fill out until he is 18 months to 2 years of age. Female shorthairs that have not been spayed will likely experience a heat cycle by the time they are a year old. Mental maturity can occur within the first year, but it is not uncommon for this to be a bit delayed, sometimes until 3 years of age.

Chapter Five

Living with a German Shorthaired Pointer

T he GSP is an exceptionally intelligent, energetic, loving, and enthusiastic companion. He is bold and friendly, especially with people. Social GSPs, however, aren't created in a vacuum. It takes an owner who is willing to work with his or her dog to develop the shorthair's true social potential. Those who take the time to socialize their dogs will possess a GSP that people will marvel at and want to meet.

German Shorthaired Pointer Behavior

The GSP was bred to be a top-notch gundog, to hunt in all types of terrain and weather, and, if necessary, provide protection to his owner. In creating this type of dog, the developers of the GSP created perhaps the most versatile, all-purpose dog known to man.

This, of course, presents its own unique challenges when it comes to socializing your shorthair. The GSP combines the drives of an intensely focused hunting dog with the potential for some guarding-breed characteristics. The intensity of an individual shorthair puppy's drives and characteristics affect his potential temperament as an adult but will vary widely from litter to litter and less widely from puppy to puppy within the litter.

In addition to the inherited blueprint for the puppy's genetic character, there is another huge force that affects how a puppy's temperament develops as an adult: the environment in which the puppy is raised. The experiences a puppy is exposed to, both good and bad, play an enormous role in shaping his final temperament.

Basically, each pup is born with the genetic potential to develop into a dog with certain characteristics and drives. The manner in which the puppy is raised with people, other dogs, and life experiences can either greatly improve upon the pup's genetic potential or damage it severely.

Socialization (done right) gives an already friendly-by-nature dog the confidence and experience to be an exceptionally mannered and outgoing adult. If an otherwise-friendly dog were kept isolated and away from people and animals, it would be unreasonable to expect him to know what to do when he finally met a person or another dog.

Your goal as the pup's owner, therefore, is to enhance the pup's good qualities, drives, and characteristics and develop him to his full potential as a social, friendly, well-adjusted adult dog through positive, high-quality experiences. The key to this is to ensure that every experience that your GSP has with people is a happy, relaxed, positive one. And the only way to make this happen is to be keenly aware of when your puppy or adult shorthair is relaxed and when he is stressed. Ideally, the shorthair would never be stressed, but if you recognize early, subtle signs of stress and address them appropriately, you can make sure the experience remains positive.

Reading Your Shorthair's Body Language

Fear biting is the number one cause of dog bites, and it happens because a dog is put in a position where he feels he cannot escape the situation and his only recourse is to bite to get away from what is scaring him so terribly.

The biggest mistake dog owners make is not recognizing the moment their puppy or dog becomes stressed and allowing the situation to progress until the shorthair is frightened enough to bite. Then the owner swears, "The bite came out of nowhere!" Wrong. The shorthair gave the owner plenty of warning, but the owner was either unaware of what was happening or was inattentive.

The same is true with dog-dog interactions. Bites do not come out of nowhere, and if an owner has socialized his GSP well with other dogs while the pup is growing up and knows his shorthair's behaviors, there will be no unexpected dogfights.

The key to all of this is to be aware of your shorthair's relaxed and friendly body language versus the first signs of stress. (See

"Personality Pointers" on page 72 for a complete description of a GSP's body language.) It's also important to be aware of the body language you most want to avoid: the shift to either fear (and fear aggression) or aggression. If a shorthair exhibits these more extreme behaviors, this is considered a "bad" experience for the dog (and most likely for you, too) that may take weeks, months, or years to fully overcome, if he ever does.

The good news is that GSP puppies are adorable, active, and cute. You will not have any trouble finding volunteers to pet them. The more you introduce your GSP puppy to strangers for pats and positive reinforcement, the friendlier he will be. (Do be careful with children, though, as they can hurt the puppy without realizing it and create a bad experience.)

Although GSP adults are more "formed," they will respond to positive experiences and continue to develop their social skills even after adulthood. Be particularly observant of an adopted adult GSP's body language and transitions before you introduce him to complete strangers. He should also already have had time to bond with you and be able to trust you when you tell him, "It's okay."

The Art of Socialization

So, you understand the importance of keeping all meetings with your short-hair positive and friendly. You understand that it's really not the quantity of positive experiences but the quality of the experiences, avoiding stress at all costs. You also understand the early signs of stress—but what in the world do you do if your shorthair starts getting stressed?

Here's the quick-start formula to avoiding stress in meetings with people and keeping things positive in both on-leash and off-leash settings.

On-Leash

Most socialization with people occurs while the puppy or adult dog is on-leash. You will be out on a walk and a friendly neighbor is approaching. Your pup has never met this neighbor before and she is a friendly sort, so things should go just fine. Your puppy is relaxed and interested in meeting this new person, so you proceed down the street and say a friendly greeting to her. Then your neighbor asks if she can say hi to your new puppy.

Here are the rules for keeping things friendly and relaxed.

Rule 1: Keep the leash loose. Whether your dog is a puppy or an adult, tightening up your leash in anticipation of your shorthair either jumping up on the neighbor or shying away means you've just sent a stress signal to your dog. Keep the leash with a slight slack in it. (Of course, this means your puppy or adult will need to know how to walk nicely; see page 126.) Also, never pull a puppy to greet a stranger. If a puppy has put on the brakes, he is beyond stressed—he is terrified. Give him as much space as he needs from the approaching person to feel comfortable and resume his relaxed behaviors.

PERSONALITY POINTERS
German Shorthaired Pointer Body Language

Mood	Friendly, Relaxed	Stressed
Head carriage	Held at a comfortable, relaxed position; relaxed (not taut) neck.	Head may drop or rise slightly; neck may appear to tighten.
Eyes	Bright, alert, and with an overall happy expression	Averting from the stressful situation; dilated pupils; increased blinking; tightened eyelids, which give the eyes a narrowing expression.
Ears	Relaxed against head or, if interested in something, softly pricked.	Alert and forward in a nervous manner or shift to a pinning against the neck.
Mouth	Open and panting easily if warm or closed if comfortable, but usually open and frequently giving licks; overall appearance is relaxed and gentle.	If open and panting, mouth shuts abruptly; if mouth is shut, the dog could begin panting if there is enough stress present to make him anxious. Other signs of stress: yawning, lip licking, drooling.
Body	Loose and relaxed; if very excited and happy, it could be wriggling; playful behaviors include dropping the chest down to the ground while keeping the haunches up (play bow).	Begins to visibly tighten. Other signs of stress: a full body shake, stretching, scratching, clawing at the owner, puppy asking to be picked up as if panicked.
Tail	Wags loosely and is held lower and wagging or higher (but not as high as on point) and wagging loosely and regularly.	Wagging slows or stops; or wagging becomes sporadic.
Voice	Usually quiet, but may bark, whine, or moan in a happy manner if they recognize someone they love and want attention.	Often silent but the dog may whimper, whine, cry, or bark in a nervous manner.

Fearful	Aggressive
Lowers and gives the appearance of cringing. (This is different from the lowering and "pointing" of the dog toward game; see below.)	Held high and erect with a tight, hard neck, or head may lower in a stiff, threatening posture.
Averting eyes and head to avoid direct eye contact; looking upward from a distinctly lowered head; pupils dilated; half-moon eye, in which the dog looks away without moving his head; tightening of eyelids.	Hard, direct, penetrating stare; dilated pupils; narrowing or tightening of eyes in a distinctly aggressive appearance.
Rotated backward and pinned against the neck.	Pricked, excessively forward, and taut.
Panting becomes more rapid and nervous; lips are drawn back during panting and give a nervous look to the dog's mouth.	Mouth closes and gives a hard appearance; lips may pull back to expose teeth in a taut snarl, or lips may push forward.
Tightens and may begin trembling; cringing or crouching; piloerection (hair is raised from neck to base of tail); submissive urination; flopping over to expose the belly.	Tense and taut as if on point but with a different intention and a unique hardness to the dog's features; possible piloerection; may progress to swift lunging or charging while snapping.
May wag but is held very low or completely tucked against the dog's rear end.	As high and hard as it possibly can be and is stiff at the base; often wagging in a very stiff, arrhythmic manner.
Silent or whimpering/crying; may also bark as the dog transitions again into fear aggression.	Silent or growling, snarling and barking with a distinctly deep and serious bark.

Rule 2: Allow the shorthair to make the approach. For most shorthairs, the preferred approach to a new, friendly human may be a full-out run with a lunge, and tons of licks. For these boisterous, I-know-no-strangers types of GSPs, teaching a *sit* (see page 121) is vital to keeping your shorthair's exuberance contained without pulling back harshly on his leash and confusing him. He will quickly learn that *"Sit"* means he gets to meet the stranger and maybe even get a cookie. Very quickly, you may find that your shorthair is sitting for pats before you even ask him. He knows how to work this crowd!

On the other hand, if your shorthair is a little more wary of strangers (even your friendly neighbor), then it is important to follow his lead and allow him to make the approach. Remember: As long as he has friendly body language, allow him to meet the person. If he shows any signs of stress or hesitation, allow your shorthair to come back to you and reconsider the situation. The key is to give your shorthair enough space from the person to get comfortable and relaxed before starting the greeting again.

Breed Needs

A Sit Caution

If you are training your puppy for field work (whether as a personal hunter or at a competitive level) or are preparing for the show ring, teaching a young shorthair to sit will be confusing. It is very bad form for a stressed GSP to sit while on point in the field (which can happen if the dog is young, stressed, confused, and trying to please you). It is also bad form for a show dog to accidentally *sit* for the judge instead of stand with his paws perfectly placed. A way around this is to teach the excitable puppy the *stand* command for greeting strangers. This is a bit more difficult to teach to an excitable shorthair, but it will save you much consternation in the field and/or show ring later.

Rule 3: Control the greeting from the human. If your shorthair is more reserved in his meetings with people, that's okay as long as he's not stressed. Help him relax by coaching the strangers in how to greet him.

- Give the person a treat and have the person hold the treat out to the pup. This controls two things—the person becomes stationary and the puppy is able to make the approach, and the person will offer the treat instead of trying to pat the puppy.
- Ask that strangers extend their hands with fingers and palm up and that if they touch the dog, to scratch him under his chin. ("That's his favorite place to be scratched!") This move is less aggressive than what most people do, which is to reach over the dog to pat him on his head.
- Approach only those friendly strangers that your shorthair doesn't mind approaching. If a person unnerves him, take him as far away as he needs to get to observe the person in a relaxed manner. This, though at a distance, is a positive encounter.

- Keep it one-on-one. It's always better to have groups of people come up and meet the puppy one by one rather than en masse. Even a bold shorthair could be rattled by an entire class of first graders diving for him.

Rule 4: Reward good behavior. He's a shorthair. Food rewards are always appreciated. Pats and praise from you are also well loved. Even if he has someone patting him and making a big fuss over him, add your dose of praise for a happy, relaxed people greeting, too.

CAUTION

"Threatening" Human Behaviors (in a Dog's Eyes)

Most people have the best intentions when meeting your beautiful new shorthaired puppy or stopping to marvel at just how regal your adopted liver-roan adult GSP looks. Unfortunately, what are typical, friendly greeting behaviors for people are not seen as friendly to sensitive dogs. In fact, some of the behaviors by humans could be misinterpreted by a dog as aggressive. When working with your GSP's socialization skills, don't be shy about controlling the approach people have toward your shorthair!

The following are behaviors that can frighten an inexperienced or timid GSP:

- Direct eye contact
- Leaning over the dog instead of allowing the dog to approach
- Patting on top of the head or approaching the dog with fingers and palm toward the ground (it could look like a "grab" position)
- Putting a face directly in the dog's face or trying to kiss the dog
- Hugging; it's not a natural dog behavior, but people and children love to hug puppies and beautiful dogs
- Loud, booming voices
- Erratic body movements (such as a stumbling toddler, a person with a cane, an awkward gait)

Rule 5: Never hesitate to back away! If you see any sign of stress, back your puppy or dog away from the person. Owners have the hardest time doing this, because it is embarrassing to have a dog that is not a social butterfly, but you shouldn't be embarrassed. It is critical that you be your dog's ambassador and that you allow only positive greetings. Sometimes, the moment of uncertainty (stress) from your shorthair may be temporary. If he shows positive, relaxed behaviors and wants to greet the person when relaxed, that's fine. Proceed as normal. If you know a certain person or a person dressed in a certain way will stress your dog (for example, someone wearing a ball cap and a puffy jacket) and you know your dog's "bubble" (the distance at which anything scary or unusual can pass by you without your shorthair showing signs of stress), then keep that bubble between you and most people—unless your dog is excited and happy to meet someone. Then you can encourage the greeting; otherwise, your goal is to get your shorthair to be more relaxed and confident around those who previously stressed him by slowly decreasing the distance he needs between him and the person.

Off-Leash

Off-leash meetings are typically less challenging than on-leash, because the puppy or adult has full control over the greeting. He is not being restrained and can check out the stranger on his own terms and at his own pace. The most common place for your shorthair to meet strangers while off-leash is in your home.

The importance of in-home meetings with new people cannot be emphasized enough for the shorthair, as he must learn that if you let someone into your home, this person is a "friend." Shorthairs have a guarding background. In some dogs, this instinct is nonexistent; in others, it rivals the instincts of more traditional guard dogs. In most, the guarding instinct falls somewhere in between.

FYI: Guarding Instincts

Do not worry that socializing your shorthair in the home will lessen his guarding instincts. This is a fallacy. The best guard dog is one that is friendly, relaxed, and confident around strangers of all ages and types. This is the only way a guard dog will be able to make the keen determination between "good" and "bad." Otherwise, if unsocialized, the shorthair with strong guarding instincts will put all strangers into the "bad" category, and then you will be a prisoner in your own house, resorting to crating your GSP anytime someone comes over because he simply won't allow it.

Having people come into your home regularly to meet and greet a young puppy is a perfect situation. If you have children, make sure their friends come over and know how to meet and greet the puppy and maybe even have the puppy perform a task for a cookie. (Having kids give the puppy the *sit* command for a treat is always a winner, as is *shake* and other tricks.) You want your GSP used to all the regular faces and people and know that good people are okay in the home.

If your GSP tends to be a hurtling ball of enthusiastic kissing, work on teaching him the *sit* command (page 121) so that you have control over him at the front door. You don't want him knocking down a frail visitor or scaring off the neighborhood kids with his wild (but well-intentioned) reckless abandon, which can, unfortunately, escalate into nipping during greetings if not controlled early on.

Keep a jar of cookies near the front door and in other rooms, and allow visitors to give your shorthair a treat if he is happy and relaxed. If you have a shy or timid dog, advise visitors to sit down and ignore the dog or puppy. Have them hold a treat and release it to the dog only when you say so. That way, you can ensure that the shorthair is rewarded when he's relaxed and not still showing signs of being stressed.

CHECKLIST

Socialization with People, Places, and Things

✔ Has your puppy been vaccinated to protect him?

✔ Are you letting your puppy get used to his surroundings first, before greeting new people?

✔ Are you keeping the number of people meeting him to a nonthreatening amount?

✔ Do you have cookies for rewarding and encouraging friendly behavior?

✔ Are you going to different places? Most pet stores welcome leashed, reasonably behaved pets. So do some outdoor cafés, coffee shops, and retail stores. Kids' sporting events, such as soccer games, typically allow leashed pets. Another good place to try is a strip mall or outdoor shopping mall.

✔ Are you giving your puppy lots of love and attention for being good?

Every Meeting Counts

GSPs are very intelligent, and will remember bad experiences as well as good experiences. It is more important to avoid a bad experience than to think that going through one will "teach" your GSP something. (Forcing him through a bad experience will teach him not to trust you, and you don't want that!)

Fortunately, the vast, vast majority of GSPs are bold, friendly dogs that take to socialization easily. But if you have the occasional more reserved (or shy) GSP, remember to go slowly and *always* with positive reinforcement. You will not change the fundamental nature of a dog any more than you will a person. A GSP that launches himself toward strangers for pats will never be reserved (although it is hoped that he will learn better manners), and a reserved GSP will never become a wild man—but they can all be good canine companions that are trustworthy in a variety of social settings.

Children and GSPs

GSPs, as a rule, are very good with children; however, all play between puppies and children should be carefully supervised at all times, and children need to know that there's no poking, pinching, tackling, hugging, face kissing, and so on. Given enough pain, any dog can snap at the child who inflicted it, and it really wouldn't be the dog's fault, but once a dog snaps, it's usually a one-way ticket to the shelter.

Children should also be taught early on not to take away a GSP's food. Yes, any family member should be able to remove food from a dog's mouth—but that doesn't mean a dog likes it, and why risk a snap or a bite (and a lasting bad experience)? The same thing applies to chew toys and bones—teach your children to let the dog have his chew, and when it's time to stop, to let the adult take the chew away. (And remember, it's a lot easier if you have a little "treat" to swap for that chew!) Avoid the entire situation by feeding your GSP and giving him super-yummy treats in his crate only.

Then, of course, your child needs to know the ground rules for the short-hair's crate—it's his, not the child's. The child should never be allowed to go in the crate with (or without) the dog.

Interaction with Other Dogs

German Shorthaired Pointers can play very nicely with other dogs, but this is not a trait that they are particularly known for. Unneutered (whole) males can be quite aggressive toward other unneutered males. Neutered males are typically everyone's friend. Females will usually play with neutered males and other females, but they will sometimes snarl and slam an unneutered male to the ground just to reinforce the concept that he'd better not get any ideas.

If you have a puppy, you'll have fun allowing him to play in puppy groups with other vaccinated puppies his size. Some training clubs offer puppy socialization classes along with some beginning puppy training. Your best bet may be to seek out friendly, relaxed adult dogs or a friendly puppy of your pup's approximate size and have a one-on-one play session.

To keep play positive between puppies (and adults), follow these rules.

1. **Keep it equal.** Similar size and play styles are important. Shorthairs tend to be big into body slamming, neck biting, and hard, fast running that other breeds may find offensive. Try to keep similar play styles together and don't let your shorthair intimidate other dogs—or allow other dogs to intimidate your shorthair (particularly a puppy).
2. **Keep it balanced.** Remember those signs of stress? The same stressors will appear in your shorthair if he's not having a good time. This is the moment to call him out of the playgroup and just watch for a while. The same goes if you see that your shorthair is causing another dog stress; call him out and have him settle down for a little while.
3. **Keep things moving.** Most scuffles among dogs happen when the owners have stopped watching the dogs interact and are busy chatting. Resist the urge to be social and keep walking through the yard or play area; help to keep play moving, too.
4. **Keep it even. Or odd.** Your shorthair will likely have a number of dogs that he is comfortable playing with, and more than that number will cause him stress. Know what your dog's tolerance level is, and call him out if too many dogs are starting to join the group.

5. Keep it cool. Dogs that play well will take time-outs from the play, relax, and then rejoin the fun. Younger dogs or those not so experienced in dog play may not naturally take a time-out. If this is the case, encourage your pup or dog to take a break at regular intervals.

6. Know your dog. It doesn't matter what someone else says: If you see that your shorthair is becoming stressed or is stressing another dog, remove him from the situation. Invariably right before the next big dogfight, an ignorant owner says, "Aw, they're just playing. Let them be." They may know their dogs' body language (though you are probably more of an expert now than they will ever be), but the important thing is that you know your dog. Keep it positive.

When the New GSP Is Dog No. 2

There are rarely problems with a GSP being the second dog you own. A fully grown, mature, and unneutered male can sometimes have an issue with another unneutered mature male, but (without females coming in season in your home) often these same males can be good friends.

In general, your GSPs (or GSP and other dog) will establish a pecking order. Sometimes this is fluid and depends on what is involved. For instance, an unneutered male might be the boss except when it comes to food. There, the neutered male couch potato and food thief extraordinaire reigns supreme, and the older male does not mess with him.

As with any new introduction, take your time introducing the new GSP in the home. Typically, a puppy will come in as lower in status to the older pet, and unless the pup is particularly dominant, there may never be a

discussion about which should reign as the leader. It is always advisable to keep the puppy and adult dog separate until you can see that both adult and puppy are not stressed and that the adult, in particular, is exhibiting friendly, relaxed behaviors. A good way to do this is to introduce the adult and puppy through a dog gate where they can sniff each other but back away from the gate if they are uncomfortable.

If you bring in an adult dog, take a little more care with the introductions. You should have already introduced the dogs at a neutral area and under the supervision of an experienced shelter behaviorist or a GSP rescue coordinator to make sure the dogs are compatible. Once this has been determined (and it's time to bring the new GSP home), have another family member meet you with your resident dog in a neutral area, such as a park, and walk the dogs together. Ideally, the dogs will ignore each other. Reward and praise them for good behavior. If there is any sign of stress, fear, or aggression, make the dogs walk farther apart. When they have relaxed, you can move them a little closer.

If the dogs are ignoring each other, then the same separation system should be used. Allow the dogs to see and sniff each other through a fence in the home and off-leash. Watch for any signs of aggression, stress, or fear. Your goal is to not allow any stress to escalate. Friendly behaviors should be rewarded for both dogs.

Crate both dogs when you cannot supervise. Whether they appear to be long-lost best friends or not, do not allow them to be alone together. As the leader of the family, the dogs will look to you for guidance and will not get into spats if you are a firm, gentle leader. When you're gone, all bets are off.

And, spoil the resident dog! Whether you've brought home a puppy or a rescued adult dog, make sure the resident dog thinks she is the bomb-dig-gity. Give her extra toys, extra walks, extra attention, extra treats, and extra praise. This helps to associate great things with the appearance of the new dog. All too often the resident dog gets less attention, no toys, no walks, and no treats, and possibly gets yelled at more. Don't fall into this trap where your sweet older dog becomes jealous of what the puppy or adult dog is getting—and she's not. It will involve more work, but that's okay. A smooth transition into the family is worth all the extra work.

Introductions to Other Pets

What about your new GSP and other types of pets? A puppy GSP can be introduced successfully in a household with cats, but there is no guarantee. If your GSP has the "cats are vermin" instinct, no amount of training will eliminate it, and your cats will always be in jeopardy.

GSPs can live just fine with reptiles (they ignore them.) Rabbits, being a game animal for GSPs, are not a wise choice. Your GSP will know that a rabbit is meant to be hunted, and will chew through doors if necessary to prove this point. Needless to say, birds are out. If you do not heed this advice, you will see the wire to your nice birdcage bent or chewed through and you might see a few feathers here and there. Yes, a GSP in the field is trained to bring the shot bird back to you, but trust this advice: A GSP will kill and eat that bird the moment your back is turned.

Communicating with Your GSP

Voice

Your GSP can absolutely tell the difference between an angry "NO!" and an enthusiastic "Good puppy!" It is not just the volume, although a thundering "NO!" works better than a hesitant "no"; it is also the intensity and pitch. Use your corrective "NO!" only when truly needed, for maximum impact. Use your positive voice as much as possible.

Physical Praise

The ultimate reward for your GSP is not food treats (though he might lead you to believe that) but actually your pats, rubs, and physical praise. As rough and tough as your GSP is in the field, he is also known to absolutely melt in your arms. You will find that many shorthairs (particularly puppies) love to crawl into your lap for pats and cuddles, and a particular favorite of GSPs of all ages are the infinitely wonderful tummy rubs. Each dog will have his favorite and will ask you for it. Unequivocally.

GSP Voice

Some GSPs will talk to you (barking when they're hungry or when you get home to greet you). Others will hardly say a word. It varies completely from dog to dog.

Movement

GSPs will often lead you to what they want—for instance, to the sink or their water bowl if it's empty. They will go down the hall toward the bedroom at bedtime, look back over their shoulder at you to let you know it's time for bed, and then wait for you to join them. They will look at the food container when they want dinner and then look at you to be sure you're "getting it." They will go to the door and ask to be pottied (once trained). Each dog is different, but you will learn quickly what your GSP is saying with his body language, his looks, and his expressions.

In the Field

If you hunt your GSP, you will learn what he is telling you in the field very quickly. You will be able to tell by if or how he flags (wags) his tail whether he is sure about the bird's location, is unsure, or the bird is running. (Generally, he is sure if he is "locked" on point with no tail movement. If the tail is wagging, he is not sure.) These are things that you will learn by working with him, and is communication on an entirely different level.

Chapter Six

Health and Nutrition

O verall, the German Shorthaired Pointer is a robust, healthy dog. If you've purchased a puppy from lines that test for genetic diseases, you are that much ahead of the game. Even with this hedge against genetic diseases, often what is most important in keeping your shorthair healthy is good preventive veterinary health care, veterinary attention to early symptoms of disease, and a lifetime of high-quality nutrition.

Preventive Health Care

Preventive health care includes regular, annual exams by your veterinarian and vaccinations against deadly diseases. At an annual exam, you can expect to have your shorthair examined from head to toe. Your veterinarian will examine his eyes, ears, and teeth for signs of disease or injury, as well as listen to his heart and lungs. Your dog's skin and coat will also be scrutinized, as will his paws and nails. His temperature will be taken and recorded, and his stools will be tested for the presence of worms. He will also be weighed.

If your shorthair is due for any vaccinations, he will receive them at this appointment. Puppies go through a series of vaccinations; however, this is not necessary for adult dogs. Depending on the type of vaccine, a single dose may be sufficient for a number of years.

At your annual exam, it is important to discuss with your veterinarian any additional concerns you might have with your GSP. This includes both physical and behavioral changes you might have observed in your shorthair. Owners often forget to ask their veterinarians for advice with behavioral problems, and in the past, some veterinarians may have had a limited interest in behavioral issues. Today, veterinarians are taking a keen interest in assisting their patients and their owners with behavioral issues, from simple questions about housetraining to more complex problems, such as resource guarding and leash aggression. Keep in mind that there should be no question too embarrassing to ask your veterinarian, who should serve not only as your first defense against disease but also as a resource for help with more complex issues that affect both the physical and mental health of your GSP.

Vaccines

A vaccine works by producing an immune response in a dog without actually causing the dog to be ill. Vaccines typically use either "modified live" or "killed" virus to create an immune response from the puppy or adult dog. If a "modified live" virus is used, it has been chemically altered so that it cannot cause a full-blown case of the disease and is self-limiting. A "killed" virus is one that has been deactivated and cannot reproduce itself at all. Live-virus vaccines can produce lifelong immunity to viruses; however, these are not safe in a dog with a compromised immune system. Killed-virus vaccines are safer for those dogs with weakened immune systems; however, they may require multiple doses and/or annual revaccination to maintain immunity.

Helpful Hints

If your shorthair is exhibiting a symptom intermittently (for example, he has an odd cough that occurs only sometimes, or he hangs his head strangely but only occasionally), and he isn't likely to replicate it for your veterinarian, whip out your cell phone and take a video recording of the symptom in action. Your veterinarian will appreciate the recording, because he or she will be able to see and hear accurately what you are trying to describe.

Vaccines can cause adverse reactions in some dogs. The most typical reaction is an allergic response, which can range from mild itching and scratching to an anaphylaxis (swelling of the airways) response. For this reason, you may be asked to remain in the veterinary office for 30 minutes after your puppy or adult has received his initial vaccinations to ensure that he does not have an allergic response. Dogs with an allergic response are treated with epinephrine, corticosteroids, and antihistamines, depending on the nature and severity of the reaction. A dog with a history of prior allergic reaction(s) may require premedicating with an oral dose of an antihistamine such as diphenylhydramine hydrochloride (such as Benadryl or its generic equivalent).

Vaccines also fall under two schedules: core and noncore. Core vaccinations are those that are considered essential to the health and well-being of your dog. Studies are finding that once the puppy series is completed and the adult dog has received an annual vaccination, the immune response lasts far longer than originally estimated. Instead of annual vaccinations, you will find that most veterinarians are recommending that vaccinations be given every three years or at even longer intervals.

One vaccine that does change and may require a more frequent or erratic schedule is the one for canine parvovirus. The reason for this is that the virus has been known to mutate, making the previous vaccination inefficient. If the virus has mutated and a new vaccine has been produced, your veterinarian will alert you to this and it may be necessary to revaccinate your shorthair.

HOME BASICS
Core Vaccines Timetable

Vaccination	6 Weeks	10 Weeks	14 Weeks	Booster	Adult Revaccination
Canine Adenovirus-2	X	X	X		
Canine Distemper	X	X	X		Every three years or longer
Canine Parvovirus	X	X	X	One year after completion of puppy vaccinations	Every three years or longer; however, this virus mutates regularly, and a new mutation means your dog will need revaccination for the new form. Consult with your veterinarian for more information.
Parainfluenza Virus	X	X	X		
Canine Influenza*	X	X			Annual revaccination with a single dose is recommended.
Bordetella*	X	X		One year after completion, or up to every six months for dogs that are frequently in high-risk environments, such as field trials, hunt tests, dog shows, etc.	Every six months for high-risk dogs; annually for lower-risk dogs. Often required by boarding kennels, training clubs, and so on.
Rabies			X	One year after puppy vaccination	Depending on local laws, revaccination is annually or every three years.

*These vaccines are not considered core vaccines; however, they are listed here because virtually all boarding kennels, training facilities, and dog parks require them.

FYI: Noncore Vaccines

Vaccination for	May be advisable for
Leptospirosis	Hunting dogs that may come in contact with soil, lakes, ponds, streams that have been contaminated with cattle, horses, pigs, rodents, wild animals, or dogs infected with leptospirosis
Rattlesnake Bites	Hunting dogs that come across rattlesnakes in the field. This vaccine is licensed for use against the effects of Western Diamondback rattlesnakes but may offer cross-protection against up to 15 species. The vaccine is designed to fight off "intoxication" from the venom, rather than an infection.
Lyme Disease	The efficacy and potential side effects of this vaccine should be weighed against the dog's need for this vaccine, particularly if effective topical tick preventives are used as a safeguard against ticks.
Giardia	This vaccine does *not* prevent infection from the parasite *Giardia*; it limits the spread of disease in a kennel of dogs. This vaccine is not recommended for companion dogs.
Periodontal Disease	This vaccine was discontinued in 2011 because of efficacy issues.

Noncore vaccinations are those that are not recommended for the entire dog population, because they are either more specific to diseases in certain locations or under certain circumstances, or the efficacy of the vaccination has not been determined. With this said, as a hunting dog, your shorthair will be exposed to more unusual circumstances than the average pet dog, and it will behoove you to discuss the noncore vaccinations that are available to you, as well as the risks involved with the various noncore vaccinations.

Parasites

An active shorthair, whether he's regularly hunted or not, will come in contact with a variety of parasites both internal and external. Fortunately, all of these parasites can be either prevented completely or treated effectively. In this day and age, there's no reason for your shorthair to suffer from parasites.

Internal Parasites

Worms

Hookworms, whipworms, tapeworms, and roundworms are easily transmitted through contaminated feces and soil. They are truly everywhere. If left unbridled, the effects of worms can range from a dull coat to more severe symptoms, such as anemia, severe weight loss, vomiting, and diarrhea. A simple fecal exam performed by your veterinarian can detect the presence of worms, and treatment is also relatively simple and efficient.

An infestation of the most common types of worms can be prevented with the regular use of a broad-spectrum heartworm preventive.

Heartworms are worms that are not transmitted through contaminated soil or feces but rather are transmitted by infected mosquitoes. No matter where you live in the United States, heartworms are present in your area. In fact, heartworms are a year-round threat in most areas. Symptoms of heartworm infestation include a cough, listlessness, and weight loss. Infestations often are fatal, because the adult worms reside in the infected dog's heart and lungs.

Heartworm infestations can be treated, but treatment is costly and carries significant risks for the dog. (If the infestation is not treated, the affected dog may not have much chance for long-term survival.)

Avoiding heartworms is safe and easy through the use of a monthly heartworm preventive, which can be given orally (and usually is snapped up eagerly by the shorthair as a yummy treat). It is also possible to prevent a heartworm infestation with a topical heartworm preventive. Both types of preventive—oral and topical—are prescription medications. A blood sample is required annually to test for the presence of heartworms before receiving a prescription for heartworm preventive from your veterinarian.

Protozoa

Protozoa are microscopic organisms that can be particularly damaging to hunting dogs that are more likely to come in contact with these organisms in the field and to become infected through ingesting diseased animals or stools, or drinking infected water. There are several different protozoan parasites that can wreak havoc, but most announce their presence with explosive, watery stools.

A protozoan infection can become quite serious in a short amount of time and requires veterinary attention, as the only way to rid the dog of the infec-

FYI: Heartworm Preventives

Some heartworm preventives can also protect against roundworms, whipworms, and hookworms; which worms the preventive combats varies with the manufacturer. Topical heartworm preventives can help control fleas, ticks, and ear mites, as well as specific worms.

tion is through prescription medications. Protozoa are zoonotic (can induce disease in humans), so make sure to take proper hygienic efforts to protect family members, too.

External: Fleas, Ticks, and Mange

The more active outdoors you are with your shorthair, the more likely he is to come in contact with fleas and ticks. (Mange is another story; more on that in a moment.) For now, the discussion is on the primary bloodsuckers: fleas and ticks.

Fleas

Cool fact: A flea can bite 400 times in a 24-hour period, and a female flea can lay up to 2,000 eggs. Okay, not so cool if those statistics apply to the fleas on your shorthair. The basic rule is that if you find flea dirt on your GSP, you've got a problem even if you can't find a flea. Flea dirt is easily differentiated from normal dirt in that if you wet flea dirt, it melts into a little red blob because it contains blood. Flea dirt is most easily spotted on your dog's back right at the base of his tail; however, you may also find it in other areas.

Treating a flea infestation requires a multipronged approach: dog, bedding/house, and yard. For the dog, use a medicated flea dip or shampoo and follow it up with a monthly, topical prescription flea preventive from your veterinarian. For the house, vacuum all surfaces thoroughly on a weekly schedule for at least a month and dispose of the vacuum bag immediately after vacuuming. (It's advisable to seal the bag in an airtight bag so any flea larvae that hatch cannot escape.) Additionally, wash all bedding in a sanitary cycle and replace any dog-bed cushions or padding that can't be washed. In the yard, mow. Mow regularly and keep that grass short to discourage it from becoming a safe harbor for fleas. In serious cases, lawns can be treated with chemicals to kill off flea infestations; however, many of these chemicals are toxic to dogs, too, and care needs to be taken in abiding by instructions for pet and human safety.

Ticks

Though most dog owners know that the deer tick can expose your shorthair to Lyme disease, there are actually several different types of ticks that can cause serious diseases in dogs: canine ehrlichiosis, canine anaplasmosis,

and Rocky Mountain spotted fever. It seems as if no matter where you live, there's probably a tick and a disease that could affect your active shorthair. So, what to do? Use a monthly topical prescription tick preventive and be vigilant in searching for ticks on your dog after every outdoor outing. (Note, too, that some topical heartworm preventives kill or immobilize ticks.)

Mange

The two most common forms of mange are demodotic mange (caused by the *Demodes canis* mite that lives in hair follicles) and sarcoptic mange, or scabies (caused by *Sarcoptes scabiei canis* that burrow into the skin). Demodotic mange is most common in young dogs or those that are under stress, are suffering from disease, and/or have been eating a poor diet. This is the type of mange often found on ill-treated shorthairs that end up in shelters or rescues and is considered noncontagious in immunocompetent adults; however, it can be highly contagious in puppies. Treatment involves the use of a broad-spectrum antiparasitic agent, such as Ivermectin.

Sarcoptic mange is highly contagious to other dogs and humans. Treatment involves parasitical treatments prescribed by your veterinarian, patience, and persistence.

Spay/Neuter

The only way to ensure that your shorthair will not be a partner in an unplanned and unwanted mating is to spay or neuter the dog. Intact male shorthairs have shown incredible athletic ability and determination in scaling or digging under fences to access a female dog in season. Female shorthairs in season may not be nearly as eager to leave the home; however, don't think that your 6-foot (1.8 m) privacy fence is necessarily sufficient to keep a budding suitor away from your female.

If you have both an intact female and an intact male, prepare for at least two weeks of sheer insanity. The howling, barking, and frantic kennel antics of the male (and female) dogs in their respective crates is enough to drive anyone insane. It takes great resolve and determination to keep intact dogs safely apart and is a very convincing argument for the spaying/neutering of at least one of the dogs.

BE PREPARED! Spay/Neuter Risks and Benefits

Male	Female
Benefits	**Benefits**
+ may reduce territorial marking indoors	+ eliminates the need for sanitary diapers, crating, pee pads in crates, washing padding, etc.
+ may reduce aggression toward other dogs	+ no more hormonal mood swings
+ no risk of testicular cancer	+ greatly reduces the risk of cancerous mammary tumors
+ reduces risk of noncancerous prostate disorders, which occur in 80 percent of intact dogs over the age of five	+ greatly reduces the risk of pyometra, which occurs in 23 percent of intact female dogs
+ may reduce the risk of diabetes	
Risks	**Risks**
	Increases risk of urinary spay incontinence
Risk of hypothyroidism triples	
Risk of obesity increases	
Risk of adverse reaction to vaccinations increases	

Unless you plan to show your shorthair in conformation, where he would need to be intact, or compete in field trials or hunt tests and have an avid interest in bettering the breed and potentially breeding your GSP at some point (after the appropriate health tests, of course), there are few compelling reasons not to alter your shorthair. If you need more information on the topic with pros and cons listed, see "Be Prepared: Spay/Neuter Risks and Benefits," above.

GSP Diseases and Disorders

The German Shorthaired Pointer has traditionally been a very healthy, stalwart dog. As the breed has climbed in popularity, the increase in certain diseases and conditions has become more apparent. Does this imply that the shorthair is plagued with genetic diseases or has a predisposition to an abnormal number of serious health conditions?

No. This is simply a list of diseases, conditions, and disorders that are seen in the shorthair with enough frequency to imply that the particular condition is significant for the breed. Some of these conditions have been shown to have an inheritance factor; others may be suspected but are not proven at this time, and still others have no apparent inheritance factor.

The GSP owner needs to be aware of the most commonly seen diseases and disorders in the shorthair, as well as the symptoms for these diseases, so that he or she can seek veterinary care as early into the disease as possible. Though many of these diseases are not curable, they are often treatable if caught early enough, which can prevent much pain and suffering for your shorthair.

Ideally, your GSP will truly be as healthy as he was bred to be and will live to a very old age. With your help and vigilant eye on changes in his health or behaviors, this will certainly give your shorthair an edge in achieving a wonderful, healthy, long life.

Eyes, Ears, and Skin

The German Shorthaired Pointer has very few hereditary disorders that involve the eyes, ears, or skin and is more likely to suffer scratches, tears, or punctures to these areas. (See "Home Basics: GSP First Aid for Cuts and Scratches," page 99.)

Eyes

The few issues that can confront a shorthair during his lifetime are as follows.

Cataracts: A cataract is the loss of transparency of the lens of the eye. Depending on the severity of the loss of vision and the dog's temperament,

the lens can be removed surgically; however, for normal visual acuity to be restored, corrective implantable intraocular lenses are required. Cataracts can be caused by a number of things, including trauma. For the shorthair, the inherited form of cataracts is called "juvenile" cataracts, which typically occur in GSPs up to about four years of age. To ensure that a shorthair is not bred with this condition, responsible breeders have their dogs' eyes tested annually and the results recorded with the Canine Eye Registration Foundation.

Progressive Retinal Atrophy (PRA): The form of PRA that GSPs are more likely to inherit is called hemeralopia or day blindness. This is a rather rare condition in which a progressive degeneration in the dog's light-sensitive cone cells (in the retina) deteriorates, leaving the dog with vision during the night but relatively or completely blind during the day and in bright light conditions. The condition has also been associated with behavioral abnormalities, because exposure to sunlight is irritating and/or painful. The disease can be diagnosed between 8 and 12 weeks of age. The disease is "autosomal recessive," so it is possible for a dog to carry the gene for the disease but not be affected by it. A genetic test is available for GSPs, and many breeders test their dogs to ensure the dog is not carrying this devastating condition.

Entropion: This condition is a common, hereditary disorder that causes a rolling inward of the lower lid (though it can also appear in the upper lid). If not corrected surgically, the lid will scratch the surface of the eye, causing painful irritation to the cornea and possibly permanent corneal damage.

Third Eyelid Abnormality: GSPs are predisposed (as a breed) to suffering from what is called "eversion of the third eyelid cartilage." (This is not quite the same as "Cherry Eye," which also affects the third eyelid, but includes a prolapsed gland.) The eversion of the cartilage causes the cartilage to curl outward and can be corrected surgically.

Ears

The GSP is fortunate in that as a breed, it does not tend to have problems with congenital deafness. Nor is the breed over-represented with ear infections. As a hunting dog, however, the shorthair does come in contact with stagnant and potentially bacteria- or fungal-contaminated water (which can wreak havoc even in a healthy ear) and is more likely (because of the heavy undergrowth he often hunts in) to have a foreign body enter and become lodged in his ear canal.

CAUTION

Bilateral Ear Infections

Usually, a dog will get an ear infection in one ear or the other. If your shorthair is getting ear infections regularly and seasonally, and the ear infections are in both ears (and rarely, if ever, in just one ear), you may be dealing with allergies.

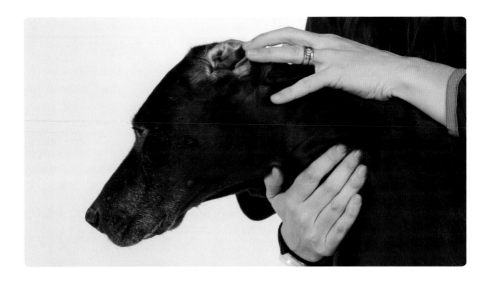

Infections: Ear infections are usually easy to spot. The dog will flap his ears, shake his head, and/or scratch his ear. When you flip the flap up, the flap will be red and hot, the ear may have a bloody, green discharge, the canal could be swollen shut, and you may be knocked over by the smell. You can gently clean your dog's ear with an antiseptic rinse; however, you will need to take your shorthair to the veterinarian promptly. Depending on the extent of the ear infection, your veterinarian may prescribe antibiotic or antifungal drops or ointment, a topical steroid to reduce the swelling in the ear canal so the antibiotic can get in the ear, an oral antibiotic, and possibly even an oral steroid, such as prednisone. Ear infections are serious, and chronic ear infections can cause serious and lasting damage.

Foreign Bodies: Another cause of great pain and often an ear infection is a foreign body. The symptoms will be very similar to those of an ear infection, and only your veterinarian will be able to get an appropriate look into your dog's ear canals to find the offending material.

Skin

Good, healthy skin accompanies a well-groomed, well-fed, healthy shorthair. If a shorthair isn't brushed and/or is fed garbage instead of healthful, high-quality food, it is possible for his skin to become dry or overly oily and flake with dander. Unfortunately, there is a disorder that has recently been seen in shorthairs, called lupoid dermatosis.

Lupoid Dermatosis: It is not known if this disease is inherited, because not enough studies have been carried out to make that determination. What is known is that it seems to affect young GSPs, and changes in the skin are usually observed by the time the pup is six months old. The skin becomes inflamed, with scaly, crusty lesions on the pup's head, lower legs, and, in males, on the scrotum. The GSP's toenails may fall out, and some dogs

HOME BASICS
GSP First Aid for Cuts and Scratches

If the scratch or cut is light, don't leave it up to your shorthair to clean himself. Carefully scrub the area with soap and water. Rinse it thoroughly and then wash it again with a betadine (povidone-iodine) solution. Dry with a clean cloth and apply a thin layer of triple antibiotic ointment to the area.

Punctures should be washed thoroughly as for scratches and cuts; however, watch carefully for any signs of infection. Punctures are much more prone to infection than open scrapes, and your veterinarian may want to prescribe an oral antibiotic as a precaution.

Deeper cuts should be cleaned thoroughly as described; however, if stitches are required, don't delay going to your veterinarian or the emergency veterinarian. The edges of the wound will begin to die, and some types of cuts (a V-shaped tear, for example) may have a small window of time in which to preserve the skin.

With severe injuries and profuse bleeding, apply pressure on the wound and have someone drive you to the nearest veterinary medical center. Note: If you are out hunting or in a different area, it is always wise to look up nearby veterinary resources and store these numbers before you begin your hunt or journey.

become ill with a fever and swollen lymph nodes. Veterinary dermatologists have taken varying approaches to treating the disease, but at this point, no known treatment is uniformly effective.

Hereditary Diseases

The German Shorthair Pointer is one of those rare breeds that despite its popularity is still robustly healthy. Conscientious breeders should largely be credited with maintaining the breed's healthy disposition. The following are known hereditary diseases or conditions that appear in the GSP.

Acral Mutilation Syndrome: This syndrome is a recessive inherited condition that affects the pain sensation in a dog's toes. Early symptoms include licking and chewing of swollen and ulcerated paws (usually the hind legs) without any apparent pain recognition from the pup. The dog may also have paronychia, a skin infection around the nails. There is no known cure at this time.

Aortic Stenosis (AS): This is a common, inherited heart condition among many breeds but is seen as a mild risk in the GSP. Of course, if your shorthair is the one to have inherited this disease, it doesn't matter if he is in the minority. In AS, the flow of blood to the left ventricle is partially obstructed, which makes the heart work harder. A shorthair with a mild

FYI: Gastric Dilation-Volvulus (GDV) or Bloat

The GSP is not at an elevated or exceptionally high risk for GDV, but he is a breed that is susceptible to this condition, so it is important that owners be aware of this disease, what it does, the symptoms, and most of all, ways to lessen the chances of their dog suffering from it.

What it is

GDV is the condition in which a dog's stomach becomes distended with gas (gastric dilation). When the stomach fills with gas and then twists, it becomes Gastric Dilation Volvulus. The twisting is deadly, as it restricts the flow of gases, fluids, and food from moving into the intestines. This torsion also cuts off the flow of blood between the stomach and upper intestines, causing the tissues of the stomach to begin to die. If a dog with GDV is not seen immediately by a veterinarian and if surgical intervention is not performed, the GSP will die quickly and painfully.

Symptoms

- Uneasiness, restlessness, unable to lie down comfortably
- Inability to vomit (but repeatedly tries)
- Drooling
- Rapid, shallow breathing
- Pale, blue, or very red gums
- Tightness in the abdomen that can become distended or "bloated"

Prevention

Several studies dating back to the mid-2000s and earlier revealed that though there is no known preventive for this condition, there are some indicators that can help dog owners better prevent bloat from occurring.

- Feed two or more small meals a day rather than a single, large meal.
- Slow down eaters that gulp their food by placing hard rubber chew toys in the bowl with the food, forcing the dog to pick around the toys to eat.
- Allow constant access to cool, fresh water.
- Allow at least an hour after recent exercise before feeding the dog his meal.
- Observe your dog more closely for possible GDV symptoms if he is showing signs of severe fear or stress (such as during a thunderstorm).

case of AS may live a normal life. More severe cases may cause exercise intolerance and fainting, and they sometimes can be treated with beta-blocking drugs and/or medical management of congestive heart failure.

Canine Hip Dysplasia (CHD): Most dog owners are familiar with the term *hip dysplasia*, which describes the condition in which the ball portion at the upper end of a dog's femur does not fit snugly and rotate smoothly within the hip socket in the pelvis. When the ball is loose, it damages the cushioning cartilage and may induce fractures in both the ball and the

socket that heal roughly, making the ball-and-socket joint fit even more poorly. As the ball continues to damage itself and the socket, the health of the joint can degrade to the point at which it is virtually impossible for the dog to support his weight on the affected leg. Mild cases of CHD may respond well to such nonsurgical treatments as NSAIDs; joint supplements, such as glucosamine and chondroitin sulfate; vitamin C (as an anti-inflammatory); acupuncture; and chiropractic treatment.

Weight control is important for dogs with CHD, as is keeping good muscle tone to support the joint. More severe CHD may require surgery. Though expensive, both triple pelvic osteotomy and a total hip replacement are surgeries with high success rates and permanent relief from pain.

Epilepsy: The appearance of epilepsy in the GSP is a situation that is being monitored closely by conscientious breeders but is not limited to the GSP. (The Canine Epilepsy Project is a collaborative study that is searching for the genes responsible for epilepsy in dogs, with the hopes of decreasing its incidence.) There is no cure for epilepsy; however, seizures may be controlled in frequency and intensity with medications such as phenobarbital, potassium bromide, or another anti-epilepsy drug (AED).

Gangliosidosis: A rare, fatal inherited neurodegenerative disorder that has been reported in GSPs, GM2 gangliosidosis appears in shorthairs aged 6 to 12 months. Affected dogs have coarse facial features and soon develop head tremors and loss of balance, followed by a severe loss of motor function, seizures, and aggression.

Hypothyroidism: This condition is caused by a decrease in the shorthair's normal thyroid hormone activity, usually in middle to later age (four to ten years of age). Symptoms include lowered energy level, hair loss, and either dry or greasy hair. Treatment is simple and involves an appropriate dose of a pill (levothyroxine) once a day for the rest of the dog's life.

Hemivertebra: A known inherited disorder of the GSP, hemivertebra is the misshapen bony development of one or more vertebrae in the shorthair's spine. In very mild cases, the condition may never cause a dog problems, but in more severe cases, it could exert pressure on the spinal cord, causing severe pain, weakness, or the inability to walk. Severe cases such as this would require surgery.

Von Willebrand's Disease (vWD): This bleeding disorder compromises the body's ability to produce blood clots. Three levels of the disorder (Type 1, Type 2, Type 3) have been identified, with Type 1 being the most common and the least severe and Type 3 causing severe bleeding disorders. A genetic test is one way to determine the presence of the disease. VWD cannot be cured; however, the most common form, Type 1, can be managed.

Cancer

According to a recent health survey from the GSPCA, the current leading cause of deaths reported to the club was cancer, followed by an almost equal percentage of those responding listing "old age." Though this may sound alarming, statistically it may be lower than average. An estimated 50 percent of dogs ten and older die of cancer; roughly a third of dogs younger than ten have cancer listed as the cause of death. The top four reported types of cancers listed for shorthairs in the survey (i.e., mammary gland tumors, mast cell tumors, hemangiosarcoma, and osteosarcoma) are the same cancers that are most common in the general dog population.

- Mammary gland tumors: The most common type of cancer reported in the survey of GSPCA members, mammary gland tumors, or breast cancer, can have a good prognosis if detected early and treated. Although benign breast tumors are encountered in spayed females, malignant mammary tumors are unusual in female dogs spayed at a relatively early age. Malignant mammary tumors do occur in a very small percentage of male dogs just as they occur in men; however, this percentage has remained relatively static at 1 percent of all malignant mammary tumors in both species.
- Mast cell tumors: Mast cells originate in bone marrow but concentrate in peripheral tissues, such as the skin. In simple terms, mast cells are a special type of cell involved in immune function that ironically can become cancerous. Mast cell tumors are graded from Grade 1 to Grade 3 and range from relatively harmless to highly malignant. The prognosis for a shorthair depends on the grade of the tumor, whether it is caught early, and whether the tumor can be completely removed.

BE PREPARED! Subtle Signs of Cancer

You know your shorthair better than anyone else and will be able to detect the first signs that something is amiss. If you detect any of the following changes in health or behavior or more than one sign, take your GSP in immediately for a veterinary exam.

1. Lumps and bumps: These may be lipomas (harmless fatty tumors), but it's good to get every new one checked out.

2. Unusual odors: Ear infections, tooth decay, and anal-gland blockages all could be suspect. It may not be cancer, but these unusual odors are almost always a sign that something needs to be treated.

3. Odd discharges: This includes any abnormal substance that is being released from any part of your dog's anatomy.

4. Abdominal bloating: Abdominal distention could be a sign of gas and/or fluids collecting in the abdominal cavity, and whether it is caused by cancer, congenital heart failure, or any number of other causes, it needs to be examined immediately.

5. An open wound or sore that won't heal: Sometimes the dog will lick an area incessantly and cause a wound; other times the wound simply won't heal. Both instances need veterinary attention.

6. Weight loss (even if your shorthair is eating well): Unless you are trying to get your shorthair to lose weight and have switched foods, it is unlikely for him to be eating well and dropping weight.

7. Not eating well: This is a red flag for any GSP. It could be an abscessed tooth or it could be something more serious (such as abdominal obstruction), but lack of appetite is right up there with a shorthair's top emergency reasons to see the veterinarian.

8. Abnormal coughing: Healthy shorthairs don't usually cough.

9. Difficulty breathing: This is cause for concern whether the dog has any additional symptoms or not. Consult your veterinarian promptly.

10. Lethargy: Definitely *not* typical of a GSP and a sure sign that something is wrong.

11. Urinary or bowel changes (reluctance to defecate, frequent urination): There could be many different causes for this, not just early signs of cancer, but any cause for changes in urinary or bowel movements is cause for concern.

12. Blood in urine or stools: Not good and a definite sign of disease.

13. Limping: Just because you didn't see what caused the limp doesn't mean the shorthair didn't injure himself, but all limps that aren't self-resolving within a few hours or a day should be examined by your veterinarian.

14. Evidence of stress related to possible pain: Is your shorthair panting periodically (and isn't hot), restless, having difficulty getting comfortable, or exhibiting other signs of stress such as dilated pupils, whining, or even trembling? Get him to your veterinarian right away.

- Hemangiosarcoma: A slow-developing cancer of the cells that line the blood vessels and eventually cause a rupture of the tumor, severe hemorrhage, and death, hemangiosarcoma is incurable, and currently a test for early detection is not available. The cancer is said to be painless in its development, and therefore, diagnosis is usually made in the very late stages of the disease.
- Osteosarcoma: Bone cancer is often first suspected with unexplained lameness, or a swelling or masslike appearance on the dog's leg. X rays will confirm the tumor. Treatment options are still limited for this form of aggressive cancer and include amputation and chemotherapy.

Perhaps the most important point to bring away from the issue of cancer and shorthairs is that early detection for many types of cancer provides the greatest potential for a good diagnosis. Early detection, even in aggressive forms of cancer, can enable you to establish a palliative care plan to keep your shorthair comfortable as long as possible.

Dog Food Decisions

Dog food options have continued to improve in the past decade, with a range of foods being offered that are free of preservatives, dubious fillers, and questionable animal parts. You will find grain-free options, healthful choices packed with antioxidants and organic ingredients, senior foods enhanced with joint supplements, diets made of human-grade ingredients, and puppy

FYI: AAFCO Nutrient Profile and Feeding Trials

The Association of American Feed Control Officials (AAFCO) develops recommendations for nutrient profiles contained in dog food. The two profiles for dog foods are (1) puppies and nursing females, "growth or reproduction," and (2) adult dogs, "adult maintenance." Foods that meet the AAFCO's recommended nutrient profiles will have this information included on the packaging. Meeting the AAFCO nutrient profiles means the food met the minimum nutrient quantities for good health, and for those minerals and vitamins that can be toxic at higher levels, the food has not exceeded maximum recommendations.

In addition, a food may also note that it has passed an AAFCO feeding trial, which means the food not only contains the necessary levels of nutrients (proven through laboratory testing) but also has been fed to dogs in feeding trials and has ensured that the nutrients are digestible and palatable. Feeding trials are important in that a food may pass a laboratory test for its nutrient content; however, if, for example, the form of vitamin C used in a food is not easily digestible, the dog is not getting the dosage of vitamin C that he should be. Similarly, a food may be packed with nutrients—and highly digestible ones—but if the food is repulsive to a dog (hard to imagine with a shorthair but it could happen), the dog doesn't thrive on the food because he's not eating it.

"brain" foods (as if the shorthair needs to be any smarter). There are dry foods, wet foods (canned), refrigerated fresh foods, and frozen raw diets.

The aisles of pet food retailers and specialty stores are brimming with healthful, great options for your GSP and all his life stages. The following is a guide to help you navigate your way through the aisles.

Deciphering Labels

Without a doubt, when it comes to high-quality food for dogs, you do pay for what you get. These foods typically aren't cheap when it comes to price per pound. What a high-quality food will give your dog, however, is outstanding nutrition, high-grade ingredients (often human grade), palatability (it tastes good), and digestibility (vitamins, supplements, and so on, as well as the food's ingredients, are highly digestible). The quality of a food will literally show in the dog's coat, skin, and eyes.

Often, high-quality foods are so packed with nutrition that a smaller amount is appropriate for feeding. An added benefit is that a puppy or dog that is being fed a high-quality food will produce moderate amounts of firm, formed stools that are easy to clean up.

How do you know if a food is high quality or not? Meeting the AAFCO minimum nutritional recommendations and passing feeding trials is a baseline must. Price is often a guide, as it costs more to include higher-grade

FYI: Wet or Dry? Or Both?

Both wet (canned) and dry (kibble) dog foods can be healthful options for puppies and dogs. Dry foods are typically made into a dough, steamed in an extruder, and then dried. (A few manufacturers have begun to bake dog food at high temperatures instead of extruding the foods.) Dry dog foods are more easily stored, don't have to be refrigerated once opened, and can be taken on trips and for travel, and some (typically larger, crunchier kibble) may help to reduce tartar and plaque if the dog chews his food. Many shorthairs eat their food with minimal chewing, so the hard kibble doesn't provide a dental benefit.

Wet foods may be cooked before sealing in the can or cooked in the can itself. Canned foods have more moisture than kibble and can be presented as a soft mold of food, chunks with juice, or, as is becoming increasingly popular, a "humanlike" stew or meal. The high-quality canned foods of today rival that of high-quality dry foods, and many premium dog food manufacturers have both wet and dry food lines. Most dogs find the palatability of premium canned foods (especially those that contain entire chicken thighs) to be exceptional. The downside to canned foods is storage after the can is opened: The contents need to be eaten or refrigerated. Also, a full serving for an adult shorthair may be two to three cans or more a day, depending on the dog's activity level and the nutritional value and caloric content of a can of food. High-quality, premium canned foods can cost more than $2/can, whereas premium, high-quality dry foods cost less than $2/serving (based on the recommended serving of a premium, high-quality, grain-free, etc., caloric- and nutrient-dense food for a 60–75-pound [27–34 kg] dog).

So, it is more economical, typically, to feed dry foods; however, some owners like to treat their dogs with a little wet food mixed into their regular feedings. This is fine, but be forewarned with the shorthair: Once you do something, he thinks you will do it all the time.

ingredients. Labels can be misleading, but one thing is true of the ingredient list: The ingredients are listed in order of prevalence. In other words, a high-grade meat, such as beef, poultry, or fish, should be listed first. A protein "meal" is fine, as is egg and a whole range of novelty proteins, such as lamb, bison, salmon, venison, duck, and others. Avoid foods that list "animal by-products," because this allows for manufacturers to include parts of the animal other than muscle meat, such as organ meats (lungs, kidneys, heart, liver, spleen, and so on) and "cleaned" stomach and intestines (freed of their contents). (Note: The AAFCO does not allow a food defined as meat by-products to include hair, horns, teeth, and hooves as has commonly been falsely documented.)

A few additional ingredients and certifications to look for on the food label:

Antibiotic and hormone-free proteins: Why subject your pet to added antibiotics and synthetic growth hormones and the potential to develop side effects, such as possible resistance to antibiotics? A food with

antibiotic- and hormone-free meats, such as beef, chicken, turkey, duck, and others is also likely to contain high-quality muscle meats.

Grain-free foods: These foods do not contain any grains (per the label) and contain 30 percent protein. The remaining mix of these foods contains vegetables (such as carrots, celery, beets, parsley, watercress, spinach, peas, and potatoes) and fruits (such as cranberries and blueberries). Grain-free foods can be helpful for dogs with allergies to certain grains or to prevent a dog from developing an allergy to certain grains.

Quality grains: If you want a food with grain, avoid those with ground corn or wheat—these are not highly digestible and tend to be the cause of food allergies for some dogs. Instead, choose a food that has highly digestible grains, such as brown rice, barley, or oatmeal.

Organic and natural: Diets that use the "organic" label contain certified organic foods, which are regulated by the U.S. Department of Agriculture and will carry the USDA organic seal on the label. A certified organic food is one that has been certified by the USDA to contain at least 70 percent organic ingredients in the food. Organic crops are prohibited from using certain pesticides. Diets that use natural in their labeling fall under a broader definition adopted by the AAFCO that allows for an interpretation of natural that could include artificially processed ingredients.

Chelated minerals: A food that meets the AAFCO recommendations is lab tested for its nutrient contents. Not all forms of vitamins and minerals are created equally, and some minerals used in dog foods are virtually indigestible. Chelated minerals are more expensive and are highly digestible, ensuring your shorthair gets the nutrition that is listed on the label.

Prebiotics: These are natural enzymes that help to support healthy digestion.

Naturally preserved: Preservatives are necessary to prevent the fats in dry foods from becoming rancid. Avoid foods that contain artificial preservatives, such as BHA, BHT, and ethoxyquin, and look for those that use natural mixed tocopherols (a source of vitamin E) or vitamin C. (Note that the shelf life of naturally preserved dry foods is roughly half that of other dry foods (6 months as opposed to 12 months).

Feeding the Puppy

A common lament among puppy owners is that often pet-care books don't tell the puppy owner exactly how much to feed the puppy—and neither does the breeder! First, let's explain the breeder's dilemma. When feeding puppies, the breeder typically mixes up a large batch of puppy food and wets it, and then the entire litter eats until they are full and a little food is left. The breeder really doesn't have a good idea about how much your puppy is eating from that bowl.

As for the writers of these pet-care books—they don't have any idea either. In fact, they don't know the age, weight, or sex of the puppy, or what type of food the puppy is currently eating (every food varies even just in calories—a cup of one food may be equivalent to 1½ cups of another food), so it would be virtually impossible to make an accurate recommendation.

Okay, so now you know the excuses and why there isn't an exact chart for feeding pups in this book, but here are some really helpful tips in making sure you feed your pup enough and correctly.

Breed Needs

When to Make the Switch

Ask three different breeders when to switch from puppy food to adult food and you will likely get three different answers. Today's puppy foods are made for the puppy during his growth period. German Shorthaired Pointers tend to reach their full height at a year but continue to mature physically until 18 months or so. Puppy food is very high in calories, so it should not be fed to a mature, healthy adult dog; otherwise the adult dog will gain weight and become obese. So making the switch should occur at least by the time the shorthair has reached maturity at 18 months, and probably much earlier.

Make the switch gradually over a week, working in more adult food and less puppy food until he is eating entirely adult food.

1. Feed the same puppy food the breeder used and prepare it in the same way. (Young pups will still have their food moistened.) Even if your pup's breeder isn't using premium puppy food and you plan to switch it, start off with the same food. Though GSPs are known to have iron guts, don't test this out with a pup. Also, the pup will have enough stress going on to cause intestinal upset, so don't add to it by changing his food right off the bat.

2. Measure out the recommended amount on the package based on the current weight of your puppy and then add a half cup more. On the bag of every puppy food is a table of suggested feeding amounts based on the puppy's current weight. These amounts are typically on the high side (no one wants you to underfeed a pup), but if your puppy is getting ready to grow, he might be eating more than average.

3. Feed the serving plus half a cup (as the breeder used to do) to the puppy in an area where he is not challenged for food by any other dogs. (Challenges can cause a pup or an adult dog to overeat.) Allow the pup at least 20 minutes to eat as much as he wants without pressure.

4. Measure the remaining amount of food that the puppy left behind. (This can be difficult if it's moistened, but it will give you an idea.)

5. Repeat Steps 1–4 for two to three more feedings until you know how much your puppy is currently eating.

6. Feed the new amount, keeping an eye on the puppy's growth and increasing the amount he eats gradually.

FYI: Fresh Refrigerated (Cooked) and Frozen (Raw) Options

If you like the idea of fresh foods already prepared and packaged for you, an increasing number of options are available at pet food retailers in a special refrigeration section. These products expire quickly, so be sure to check the expiration date.

Additionally, a number of manufacturers sell frozen foods that are either fresh (cooked) food or raw diets. Frozen foods can be purchased both at pet food retailers and online. Raw diets are still controversial, and prepared products have been the subject of pet food recalls. Before embarking on a raw food diet, discuss with your veterinarian the benefits and challenges that come with this food preparation.

Young puppies are often fed three times a day; older puppies can do well being fed twice a day. This twice-a-day feeding routine can be continued for the life of the GSP.

Feeding the Adult

The adult male GSP weighs between 55 and 70 pounds (25–32 kg), and a female will weigh between 45 and 60 pounds (20–27 kg). Very little of this weight is "fat"; the shorthair is an exceptionally athletic breed, has a lean, muscular body, and is very active. That means that pound for pound, the adult shorthair may eat more than you are used to in a similar-sized dog.

Or not. Depends.

An active adult GSP that is being fed a high-quality, well-balanced food may do well on two cups a day—or he may require four or five cups a day. It depends on how much exercise he gets, his individual metabolism (i.e., younger versus older), what kind of weather he's training in (cold weather requires more energy than training in warm), his home life, if he enjoys stretching out on a couch or is an example of continuous motion, and so on.

If you've adopted your adult from a rescue or shelter, they will have a good idea of how much your shorthair is eating. If you have raised your GSP from a pup, you will also have a good idea of how much he is eating. What can be difficult to determine is whether your GSP is eating too much. Your dog will protest that he isn't really ever eating enough; however, we know this to be false.

To determine if your GSP is at the appropriate weight, take your fingertips and gently push on his ribs. When you gently press, you should feel his ribs through a light covering of fat. If you don't have to press, he is too thin. If you have to press a bit hard to find his ribs, then he could use some trimming down. (See "Be Prepared: Handling Obesity," page 112.)

Senior Considerations

When feeding senior GSPs, your primary concerns may revolve around how much your dog is eating. If he is overweight, he is eating too much, and exercise options, depending on his mobility, may be limited. See "Be Prepared: Handling Obesity," page 112, for more tips.

On the other hand, you may find that though your elderly shorthair is not ill, his appetite may be waning. (Remember: Be sure to rule out disease and, in particular, a bad tooth with your veterinarian!) To make your shorthair's meals more appealing, you can do the following:

- Use low-sodium beef or chicken broth to moisten his food.
- Mix in a small portion of high-quality canned food with his kibble.
- Warm your shorthair's food slightly so that it brings out the flavors and aromas.
- Feed by hand, sitting next to your shorthair. This can often be just what the dog needs to "get going," and he will polish off the rest of his meal by himself.

Homemade Diets

In 2007, perhaps the largest dog food recall occurred when a distribution company sold melamine-tainted wheat gluten to many different pet food companies. The result was a number of foods that were tainted, and

BE PREPARED! Handling Obesity

An estimated 55 percent of dogs are overweight or obese. As active as the GSP is, there are dogs that are overweight. If your shorthair needs to shed a few pounds (or more), here are a few tips.

- Reduce his food intake. Your veterinarian can recommend an appropriate amount based on your dog's current intake. A good guide is not more than a 25 percent reduction in total food. Measure his food, too. Don't guess how much a scoop is. (It's probably a lot more than you think!)
- Add no- or low-calorie healthful fillers to add bulk to your dog's smaller portions. Raw green beans, chopped raw carrots, apple, or a half cup of canned pumpkin can be good choices.
- Consider a high-quality weight-control food. Avoid cheaper varieties that have unhealthful fillers in them. Make sure the product is from a reputable producer of high-quality foods.
- Feed regular meals. Do not allow your GSP to free-feed.
- Cut out table scraps. These add up quickly, not to mention the fact that fatty foods can trigger pancreatitis.
- Replace with healthful snacks. Use baby carrots, diced raw squash, or broccoli.
- Calculate training treats. If you use chopped chicken or prepared training treats, be sure to include the calorie content of these treats *or* use your GSP's meal portion for his training sessions.
- Increase your GSP's exercise. Less food in and more calories burned equals weight loss.
- When all else fails … there is medication that can be prescribed to help control your dog's appetite (dirlotapide) and help reduce his fat absorption. The only current FDA-approved drug is Slentrol, and it is not without its side effects. Discuss your options with your veterinarian to determine whether this approach is appropriate for your GSP.

thousands of dogs and cats were either sickened or killed. Recalls haven't stopped with the 2007 episode: Recent dog food recalls have included dry dog foods, treats and chews, and raw frozen diets. The foods have been recalled for contamination with *E. coli*, excessive levels of vitamin D, salmonella, mold, a toxic chemical by-product of fungus, small melted pieces from a worker's plastic hard hat, and the list goes on.

After the sweeping effects of the 2007 pet food recall, many dog owners considered making homemade diets for their dogs. If you are considering preparing meals for your GSP, you will have control over everything that goes into your dog's system and can choose fresh, high-quality ingredients. Preparing homemade diets is not easy, and before launching into cooking

FYI: Keeping Track of Recalls

In 2009, two dog food recalls were recorded; in 2010, there were more than 13 dog food recalls; and in 2011, six recalls were recorded. After the widespread disaster of tainted wheat gluten in 2007, the U.S. Department of Health and Human Services launched a government consumer web site that includes pet food recall information at *www.foodsafety.gov* where owners can keep up on the latest recalls (for all foods).

meat loaf and mashed potatoes for your GSP every night, you should realize that there's a lot more to preparing meals properly for a dog.

- The diet must be written by a veterinary nutritionist. Balancing the nutrients in a dog's diet correctly is much more difficult than you might think. (Most recipes are actually for snacks or one-time meals rather than complete, balanced meals.)
- Do not delete or substitute. Every ingredient and every measurement is given by the veterinary nutritionist for a reason. The diet is balanced. Increasing a supplement, substituting a protein, or doubling another ingredient can lead to disaster.
- Measure, measure, measure. Did we mention measuring? This is not a matter of throw-in-a-little-of-this here, throw-in-a-little-of-that there. It is a balanced diet.
- Don't cut corners. Homemade diets can be very expensive to prepare, and sooner or later many owners decide not to purchase a vitamin or bonemeal or a certain supplement because it's too expensive. Cutting corners is said to be the number-one reason most homemade diets fail and veterinarians see malnourished, home-fed dogs in their clinics. Be committed!

A good source for homemade diets is through a board-certified veterinary nutritionist. (A board-certified veterinary nutritionist can be found through the American College of Veterinary Nutrition at *www.ACVN.org*.) You may not have this expert locally, but it is likely that your veterinarian has balanced recipes on hand that have been prepared by a board-certified veterinary nutritionist.

Another terrific source for homemade diets is the web site *www.balanceit.com* that was developed by a veterinary nutritionist and allows you to build different balanced recipes for your dog. You can build a recipe completely from scratch, using all fresh ingredients. The site allows you to choose either commonly available, human-grade vitamins, minerals, and supplements to purchase on your own or supplements sold by Balance It.

Chapter Seven

Training and Activities

The German Shorthaired Pointer is an exceptionally intelligent dog, largely because he was bred to be a multitasker. His "brain" isn't specialized for one specific task; rather, he is capable of handling many tasks at an expert level. Additionally, he was bred to think both independently (for some tasks) and in partnership with his handler (for other tasks). With any über-intelligent dog breed, you will find that training in some aspects is amazingly easy—and in some aspects you will find that his training can be amazingly challenging, too. What you won't find is that training a GSP is boring!

Training the GSP

The genetics for your shorthair were originally focused on creating a well-rounded, all-purpose hunting dog with the courage and presence to protect his handler if needed. Today's GSP continues these traditions and continues to excel as a multipurpose hunting dog as well as an amazing companion.

Keep distractions to a minimum at first. As a gundog, the GSP can become exceptionally focused and has the ability to plow through difficult terrain, endure frigid temperatures, and even suffer injuries without faltering toward his goal. This ability to focus through physical stress and pain is admirable in a hunting dog; however, it can relate to early training difficulties with a novice shorthair handler. Put simply? Basically any bird or small animal is reason to go on intense alert and completely turn off the "hearing" (i.e., that is to your voice only) and focus on the bird or critter.

Therefore, shorthair owners should begin early training in a location that is as distraction-free as possible. Choose a quiet room indoors, without family and other pets anywhere in sight, and begin your home-schooling. As the GSP learns commands and learns to listen no matter what, you can start working the well-learned commands with slight distractions. Work your way up slowly to training in the most difficult of surroundings.

Burn some energy first. To help your energetic and tireless GSP focus on training sessions, try to work him when he's not quite as full of energy.

CAUTION

Be Temperature Savvy

Adjust the length of your training sessions not only to your GSP's mental abilities but also to his physical abilities with weather as a consideration. Working well in hot summer weather requires frequent access to cool water. Working in cold weather also requires regular water and attention to your GSP's paw pads. As tough as the shorthair is, his feet will freeze, and they collect any road salts and debris left over from inclement weather in the streets and on sidewalks. Wash and dry your dog's paws thoroughly if he has been in chemically treated streets.

Young pups may do fine with a ten-minute walk, whereas an older adolescent may need a longer, brisk run.

Keep it fun and fast paced. A challenge with training intelligent dogs is that they become bored easily. Keep your training sessions moving from skill to skill, and keep it fun. If your GSP doesn't realize he's being "trained," then you are doing your job right! Young puppies do well with multiple training sessions for just a few minutes throughout the day. Older puppies and adolescents can have longer sessions—up to 15 to 20 minutes (with breaks) a couple of times a day. A very focused adult dog may be able to work 30 to 45 minutes in a session, or longer with breaks and playtime. Be careful, however, to avoid training your GSP past his abilities in terms of time. You want to end on a positive note with your shorthair wanting more (training is time with you, remember).

Work hungry. Training with treats works best if the puppy or dog is hungry. Training with treats (even for the shorthair) is not as efficient after the pup or dog has had a full meal.

Be happy and confident. Your attitude while training your GSP will have a direct influence on how well he focuses on you and how quickly he learns. If you are happy and confident and show it not only in your voice but in your body language, he will be happy and confident, too. (If you've had a bad day, put off training until another time.)

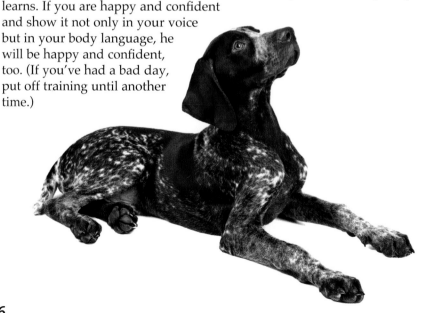

How Your GSP Learns

If you've trained dogs before, read training books, or watched one of many popular dog-training shows on television, you're probably familiar with the training term operant conditioning. Basically, operant conditioning is the process of teaching (conditioning) an animal to provide a specific behavior in response to a "cue," such as a voice command (*"Sit!"*) or a hand signal.

What many people don't realize is that operant conditioning works with both positive and negative reinforcement training. With positive reinforcement training, the dog learns to produce a behavior to receive his reward. With negative reinforcement training, the dog learns to produce a behavior to avoid something he perceives as negative.

Positive, reward-based training is the foundation for all basic training. It is more fun to train using positive, reward-based techniques, and the happy GSP is an eager learner. Negative reinforcement does have a role in advanced training (see "When Consequences Are Necessary," page 124), but harsh, forceful, physical negative reinforcement training does not have a role at any level of training!

FYI: Luring, Shaping, Capturing, Targeting: It's All Good!

An integral part of positive, reward-based training is shaping the desired behavior without ever forcing the dog into position. If you've ever tried to force an adult GSP into a *sit*, you'll understand how this concept of shaping a behavior without force came into being. Four ways of shaping a desired behavior are Luring, Free Shaping, Capturing, and Targeting.

Luring: Most dog owners are familiar with the luring technique. With luring, the owner takes a treat (or toy) and uses it to shape a behavior. For the *sit*, for example, the owner holds the dog's collar and moves the treat from the dog's nose backward toward his ears, causing the dog to follow the lure and fold into a *sit*.

Shaping: What if the behavior you are trying to shape is a little more difficult for your dog to "get" on the first try? For example, the *down* can be difficult to teach in one swoop, but if it is taught in increments, and the GSP is rewarded each time he gets a little farther down,

the *down* can be relatively easy to train. When rewards are given in increments of achievement, this is "shaping."

Capturing: When a puppy or dog provides the desired behavior on his own, you can "capture" this behavior and link it with a voice command. For example, if the puppy is running toward you, you can say, *"Come!"* right as he barrels into your legs. Reinforce the good behavior with lots of praise and you've started the capturing process.

Targeting: This shaping tool involves an actual "targeting" tool, which is much like an expandable pointer with a ball on the end. The idea is to teach the GSP to touch his nose to the end of the pointer, for which he receives a treat. Once he knows that he is to look for the target stick and touch his nose to it, the target can be used to teach such things as a "send-out" (the dog is sent away from you), as a guide through weave poles, and a myriad of other simple-to-complex behaviors.

Cue and Behavior Association

When teaching your GSP a new behavior, your goal is for him to provide the behavior quickly and confidently when you give him the cue (voice command or hand signal) for the behavior. The fastest way to teach your GSP to learn a behavior with confidence is to wait when it comes to linking the cue with the behavior.

In other words, lure or shape the behavior first (see "Luring, Shaping, Capturing, and Targeting," above), and then once you've been able to create the correct behavior, link the voice command at the moment when you are 99 percent sure he is going to produce the behavior. In other words, as you lure him to rock back in a *sit*, say, *"Sit!"* not as you hold the treat in front of his nose but as he is finishes his *sit*. In this way, he will link the final action of the *sit* with the voice command, *"Sit!"*

As he lures more quickly and confidently into the *sit,* you can back up the voice command, *"Sit!"* to his new "confidence" point—the point where you are 99 percent sure he is really going to sit. This could be halfway into the *sit.* As he continues to increase his confidence in understanding the luring and as you continue to link the command with the behavior, you can back up the cue even further: Now you can say *"Sit!"* as you hold the treat in front of his nose and just barely begin to rock him back.

What you want to avoid is the situation in which you say, *"Sit!"* first and then try to lure the dog into position (and most likely fail at the first few attempts). The GSP is smart, and just these few missteps will confuse him about what *"Sit!"* actually means. Does it mean kinda squat? Does one *"Sit!"* mean nothing but four ways to *sit?*

Remember: You don't have to say the command until you are sure you can lure or shape your GSP into the desired behavior. Once you are having success with creating the behavior, you can begin linking the command.

Learning the Basics

Your GSP does not need to have 20 or 30 commands in his repertoire to be considered a well-behaved companion. In fact, the six commands below are the foundation to an amazing pet companion.

The GSP, of course, will be happy to learn as many exercises and behaviors as you're willing to teach him and can go on to be a stellar agility dog, obedience whiz, or rally dog extraordinaire. How far you want to take your GSP with his training is up to you, but you'll find that a solid response to the *name, sit, stay, down, come,* and *walk nicely* commands will provide the building blocks for a great companion, as well as for most competitive and noncompetitive sports.

Remember, the following exercises are meant to be taught over time. A young puppy may take a few weeks to learn how to be lured into a *sit.*

Helpful Hints

What Is Clicker Training?

A very accurate way of pinpointing or "marking" the moment a dog provides a desired behavior in training is to use a "clicker." To use the clicker, you will need to make the association of the sound of a <click> with a reward. With a handful of tiny, tasty treats, <click> directly in front of your GSP and then treat him. Continue to <click> and treat, <click> and treat, and <click> and treat. The pup will pick up the connection between the sound of the <click> and receiving a food reward.

Once this relationship has been established, the clicker can be used with luring (<click> and treat the moment he *sits*), shaping (<click> and treat as he gets incrementally closer to lying all the way down for the *down*), targeting (<click> and treat when his nose touches the end of the target stick), and capturing (<click> and treat as the dog enters the kennel on his own).

For more information on clicker training, see "Resources," page 169.

An adult may learn this same skill in a few tries. The key to successful training is to teach the behaviors in small steps, setting up the puppy or adult to succeed. Make sure he is performing the exercise (at the level you are training it) with speed and confidence before you make it harder for him by either adding more time (for example, the number of seconds or minutes he stays in the *sit*), more distance (for example, that you can step away from him in the *sit-stay*), or more distractions (such as moving from performing a *sit* in a quiet kitchen to working on the same skill in a family room where a child is watching television).

When you make an exercise harder for the first time (by adding time, distance, or distractions), go back to the very first training step. So, if you've trained your puppy to *sit* when you say "*Sit!*" and you've been training in your kitchen, don't expect to go out to your front porch and pick up where you left off. Go back to luring him into a *sit*, and teach the skill all over again in the new location. Don't worry. It will go very quickly, but in this way you set up your GSP to succeed. Positive, confident, successful repetitions are much better than failed attempts or uncertain tries.

Helpful Hints

Basic Training Tools

For training, choose a leash and a collar that you use only for this purpose. When first starting out, a 4-foot (1.2 m) leash is a very controllable length and shorter than you'd use on your walks. The collar can be identical to your GSP's everyday collar (i.e., a flat buckle or quick-release collar), but the fact that it is used only for training purposes will make it special in your shorthair's eyes, and he will know it means this is different from a walk and (over time) that he is expected to focus.

Name

Every dog knows his name, right? Correct, but teaching the GSP his name in the following manner allows you to use his name to gain his focus. (It is best to confine his name to one, or at the most, two syllables.) The goal is for the GSP to hear his name, make direct eye contact with you, and wait in anticipation of his next command. To teach the name as a means of focusing your GSP, use the following steps.

1. When your GSP is looking directly at you, say his name.
2. Mark the response with a "yes!" or a <click> (if you are using a clicker and have already trained the <click> and treat response).
3. Reward the puppy with a treat and praise.
4. Repeat steps 1–3 whenever you catch your GSP looking directly at you.

5. Make it slightly harder: When your GSP is near you and not distracted, say his name and look for him to turn his eye toward you. Mark the behavior with a "yes!" or a <click>, treat, and praise. (You are now *shaping* or rewarding increments of focus when you say his name.)

6. Repeat step 5, practicing and rewarding for eye turns.

7. Continue to make it harder by rewarding a bigger response: from eye turns, to head turns, to head and shoulder turn, to eventually running directly to you.

Sit

For everyone except those training for hunt tests and field trials, the *sit* could be the most valuable tool in your training box. Hunters and trailers may not want to teach the *sit*, as a young dog in training may *sit* while he is on point in the field if he is anxious, unsure of himself, or confused, which is not unusual in the beginning stages of training.

For everyone else who owns a GSP, teach the *sit*. Teach it early and work on it often, making it fun for your GSP. This exercise can help diffuse the exuberant GSP greetings (that can knock a person down); it can be used to prevent the dog from bolting out the front door or to keep a hungry GSP from knocking a full bowl of dinner out of your hands before it reaches the floor.

There's a world of uses for the *sit* command, and fortunately, it's one of the easiest to teach.

1. Gently hold the dog's collar in one hand, and with a treat in the other hand, slowly begin passing the treat (encircled in your hand with the back of the hand nearly skimming the dog's bridge of his nose) from his nose to between his eyes and slowly toward his ears.

2. He will rock back as he lifts his chin to follow the treat and will fold into a *sit*, probably before the treat reaches his eyes.

3. Practice this a few times until he is rocking back relatively quickly and is completely in a *sit* and not squatting or trying to back up.

4. When he rocks completely into the *sit*, mark this with a "yes!" or <click> and then treat.

5. Continue practicing steps 1–4, and begin adding the command *"Sit!"* as he completes the *sit*. Then mark and treat. Work toward being able to say *"Sit!"* when the lure is in your hand at his nose. Eventually you will be able to say it without using the lure.

Stay

The command for *stay* can be taught with any position: the *sit*, the *down*, or even when the dog is in a standing position. The basic principle of the *stay* command is the same no matter the position. So, since your GSP knows his *sit*, teaching the *sit-stay* is a natural.

1. With leash attached to your GSP's collar and with your pup on your left side, put your GSP in a *sit*.
2. Make sure your GSP is sitting quietly and is rock solid.
3. Holding the leash in your right hand, pass your left hand, fingers down and palm toward the dog's nose, in a short movement from right to left directly in front of the dog's nose and say, "Stay!"

4. Stand up straight. Do not move. Remain still for several seconds.
5. Mark "no movement" with a quiet "yes!" or <click>, and then treat.
6. Resettle him and repeat steps 1–6.
7. Add movement. Repeat steps 1–3. This time, after you've said, *"Stay!"* stand back up straight and take one step out to the right with your right foot, keeping your left foot in place. (Movement of the left foot always means for the dog to move with you. Keep this foot in place.)
8. Rock immediately back into place and mark "no movement" with a quiet "yes!" or <click>, and then treat. Practice, making sure he's solid with you stepping out and stepping back in.
9. Add time. Repeat step 7, but this time when you step away, count to five and step back. Reward "no movement" with a quiet "yes!" or <click>, and then treat.
10. Continue adding distance and time (never together) until you can walk around your dog while he sits, and walk forward—always stepping forward on the right foot first to signal a *stay*. If your GSP breaks his *sit-stay* at any time, simply put him back in a *sit*, and then go back to the beginning and build up again.

Down

The *down* is an excellent command to help settle a wild puppy, allow you to eat your dinner in peace, and help confirm on a daily basis that you are in the leadership role and that the GSP is never more than second in command (or third, or fourth, or … depending on the size of your family). Because the *down* is a submissive position, some dogs are a little more resistant to going completely down. Others just have a little harder time figuring out what you're trying to get them to do. For this reason, the technique of "shaping" (see page 118) is used, in which the pup is rewarded as he makes progress toward the *down*.

1. With your GSP on-leash and in a *sit*, take a treat and slowly move it toward the floor. Go only as far down as you can without the pup's rear end popping back up.
2. Mark the GSP's movement toward the floor with a quiet "yes!" or <click>, and then treat.
3. Repeat steps 1–2 and try to get the pup to get closer to the floor, making him work a little harder for the treat. Mark his progress toward the floor with a quiet "yes!" or <click>, and then treat.
4. Continue working until (over time and this could be a few days) your GSP lies down completely, elbows to the floor. Mark the *down* with a quiet "yes!" or <click>, and then treat. Practice several times to make sure he is consistently lying all the way down.
5. Add the command *"Down!"* as he completes the *down*, and then mark the *down* with a quiet "yes!" or <click>, and then treat.

Practice, practice, practice!

FYI: When Consequences Are Necessary for the "I Don't Wanna"

Your GSP knows his stuff. He is rock solid on his *sits*, his *downs*, and his *recalls*, and he walks on a loose leash by your side. Then it happens: You're in the kitchen and you tell him to *sit* for a treat and he stares at you. He's happy. He's wagging his tail. He wants the treat. He knows what "*Sit!*" means. He's not confused. He's not unsteady. He just doesn't want to *sit*.

Now what? Why is he doing this?

He could be testing the waters to see if he really has to obey you to get that treat. Fact is, he does have to obey you. This is the time when a consequence (negative reinforcement) is needed to make sure the dog knows he must obey a command. In the case of I-don't-wanna-sit-for-my-treat, simply withhold the treat. Say, "*Hey!*" to get his attention in a stern manner. He should be sitting at this point. If not, gently reach around for his collar and rock him back with the treat as a lure. Good boy! Don't give him that treat. Repeat the exercise. Good boy! And one more time. Now he can have his treat.

With some exercises it can be more difficult to create an appropriate consequence. Skilled, experienced handlers and trainers create consequences quite naturally (such as a verbal response, "Eh! Eh!" or a quick tug on the leash). Learning when to enforce a consequence and the precise timing of the consequence can be tricky; this is where a good instructor and a training class can come in handy.

The most important point to remember is that training is entirely positive and reward-based while the GSP is learning a skill. Consequences can occur only when the GSP knows exactly what you've asked him to do and has been performing this exercise with speed and confidence.

Come

At a companion dog level, you want your GSP to come running when you call him. You want him to quit barking at that dog on the other side of the fence and get inside. If he's run out the front door after a critter, you want him to come back. If he's out playing in the dog park and it's time to go, you want your GSP to listen and get over to where you are.

These are high expectations. When a GSP is on guard duty, critter chasing, or having the time of his life, he is least likely to obey your commands. Does that mean you throw in the towel and figure you can never teach your GSP a reliable recall? No! It means you work harder. In the beginning, you set him up for success, making it almost impossible for him not to *come* if you call him. You make coming to you more fun than anything this GSP could possibly imagine. It's a game. He's always rewarded. And you don't test the waters unless it's an emergency.

Is he at the fence, barking at the neighbor dog? Don't risk saying, *"Come!"* and having him ignore you (learning that he doesn't have to *come* because you are too far away for there to be an immediate consequence for not coming). Go get him and bring him in, saying, "Let's go!" in a positive manner as he runs back in the house with you. Condition him to a cowbell. (Think of it as a big clicker and make the prize a big, jackpot reward.) As he makes the final run into the house, and you know he's coming in the back door, say, *"Come!"* (This is using the "capturing" technique; see page 118.)

There are so many ways to call a dog to you without saying *"Come!"* that you might wonder, why teach this? Because sometime you might really, really need the *come* command, and if your GSP has never, ever failed in your training when you've given him the command, odds are that when you are in an emergency situation and you say, *"Come!"* with authority, he will *come*.

Taking Every Opportunity to Teach the Come

To keep your pup or adult from ever failing to come when you call him, make sure to link the command *"Come!"* with the final action of the recall. In other words, say, *"Come!"* as your puppy flies into your arms, not when he's sniffing behind the couch and there's little chance of him even looking at you. Look for any and all opportunities to work on the *come* command.

1. While walking your GSP on-leash, start walking backward. As soon as your shorthair turns and starts trotting toward you, say *"Come!"* Praise and reward.
2. In a room or in the backyard, have a family member hold the GSP while you are not more than 10 feet (3 m) away—and doing everything silly to get your puppy to come running to you. Have your family member release the pup, and when he barrels toward you and you are certain he is coming to you, say, *"Come!"*
3. Bang the dinner dish when it's feeding time and as your hungry shorthair comes running, say, *"Come!"*
4. When playing in the yard, turn and run in the opposite direction. When you see your GSP racing toward you, turn and say, *"Come!"*
5. Take every "sure" opportunity to reinforce the *come*. Praise your GSP lavishly for coming to you.

Note: Do not undo all your good work by punishing your GSP for coming to you. Don't call him over to look at a mess he's made. He won't connect that you're angry that he chewed up a pillow; he'll think you're angry at him for coming when you called him.

Walk Nicely On-Leash

Competitive heeling requires that a dog match your pace, whether you speed up to a jog or slow down to a very slow walk. He must keep his shoulder even with your left leg as you turn corners, and make figure eights. He also must *sit* automatically, without you telling him, whenever you halt.

And as soon as you stride out with your left foot forward, he must immediately snap into heel position and move forward, too.

Heeling is awesome. It requires work and focus. It's not how you walk a dog, however. For the companion dog owner and the little puppy, your first goal is to get your shorthair to walk nicely on the leash without taking you for a drag. Once you've got the *walk nicely* started, you can work with an obedience club and work on that polished heel!

1. Burn off a little energy. You know your GSP is going to want to pull on the walk, and if he is full of energy, it will make training the *walk nicely* that much harder. If you can encourage him to chase a toy in the yard or just play chase with you for a little while, it will help in the early stages.
2. Clip on his leash (once he's calmed down a little).
3. Make sure you are carrying a motivator. This could be food with some GSPs, but for others it might need to be more important—a higher reward, such as a favorite tug toy.
4. Make sure your GSP sees you have the item in your right hand. Walk briskly and swing your right arm so he can see you've got the toy. This will encourage him to stay with you.
5. Reward him frequently with the toy as you walk.
6. Talk to him to catch his attention. Change directions frequently. Speed up. Slow down. Reward every instance in which he looks for you and changes directions with you.
7. Consider using a head halter or a no-pull harness for adolescents or adult dogs that are learning to walk nicely.

BE PREPARED! Competitive and Noncompetitive Activities for All GSPs

Activity	Special Skills?
Agility Competitive (also noncompetitive)	The athletic GSP can excel in agility; dogs should be free of hip or other musculoskeletal problems.
Conformation Competitive	A show-quality GSP; intact; trained to "gait," "stack," and "bait." May be owner-handled, but both owner and dog will need handling classes.
Flyball Competitive	GSP must not be dog-aggressive, be in good health, and ball crazy. Sport requires a team of four dogs and handlers, with each dog running a hurdle course, releasing a ball, and running back to the start.
Hunt Tests, Field Trials, etc. Competitive and noncompetitive; see Chapter 10	
Musical Freestyle Competitive	This is the sport of "dancing with dogs."
Obedience Competitive (also noncompetitive)	Every GSP should be able to attain a novice title of Companion Dog.
S.T.A.R. and Canine Good Citizen Noncompetitive	The S.T.A.R. puppy program and the Canine Good Citizen are noncompetitive programs that certify dogs and handlers in basic skills.
Rally Competitive (also noncompetitive)	This fun sport has a number of stations set up with a skill to perform at each station.
Tracking Noncompetitive	GSPs excel at tracking. Owners need to have some physical fitness to track at higher levels.
Animal-Assisted Therapy Noncompetitive; Service	The GSP's temperament must be rock solid in all types of situations and with all types of people. Certification is through one of several national organizations.
Search and Rescue Noncompetitive; Service	GSPs excel at SAR work with excellent tracking and trailing abilities.

Contact Information

American Kennel Club (AKC), Canine Performance Events (CPE), North American Dog Agility Council (NADAC), United Kennel Club (UKC), United States Dog Agility Association (USDAA)

American Kennel Club (AKC), United Kennel Club (UKC), Canadian Kennel Club (CKC)

North American Flyball Association (NAFA), United Flyball League International (U-FLI)

World Canine Freestyle Organization, Musical Dog Sport Association

American Kennel Club (AKC), United Kennel Club (UKC), Canadian Kennel Club (CKC)

American Kennel Club (AKC)

American Kennel Club (AKC), Association of Pet Dog Trainers (APDT)

American Kennel Club (AKC)

The Delta Society, Therapy Dogs International, Inc., R.E.A.D. (Reading Education Assistance Program)

National Association for Search and Rescue

10 Questions About Problem Behaviors

1 **How do I get my puppy to stop nipping?** GSP puppies are very mouthy by nature. Remember, retrieving is just one of their specialties, which means they like to carry things in their mouths. Excited puppies will extend this mouthiness to nipping. To prevent nipping, offer the pup something to carry in his mouth. (He can't nip if his mouth is full.) And, supervise his interactions with the children *at all times*. The more excited he gets, the more likely he is to behave inappropriately and nip. Have him take time-outs to settle down as needed.

2 **My GSP jumps on everyone when they come to visit. Help!** This is actually a friendly dog greeting, but it's not good house-dog manners. Teach your GSP to *sit* and require him to *sit* to receive pats from visitors. Also, consider gating him away from the front door so that you have an opportunity to allow someone in your home and then can focus your attention on introducing the puppy to your visitor.

3 **What can I do to get my GSP to stop barking at the front door?** There are two ways (at least) to approach this. (1) When you are not home, do not allow your GSP unfettered access to the front door. You can't control his self-rewarding experiences, and the barking will only get worse. Gate him away from the front door or better yet, crate him. (2) When you are home, allow him to bark briefly as you immediately check out why he is barking. Then remove him from the door to silence barking. Teaching him a solid *down* can also help to silence barking. Be sure to reward him for being quiet.

4 **My GSP lunges and growls at other dogs when we go on walks. How can I stop him?** Work on basic obedience skills (*walk nicely, sit, down, come,* etc.) in your home. When out, know your GSP's "bubble"—the distance at which he can pass another dog without showing any aggression or signs of stress. Keep a slight slack in the leash to make sure your GSP doesn't pick up on any anxiety you might have when he's about to pass another dog. Keep him active and distracted with obedience commands and throw them at him rapid-fire. This way you can reward him for good command responses. Work toward decreasing his bubble distance over time. If at any time you feel you cannot control your dog, consult a trainer immediately.

5 **My puppy urinates when my husband comes home. What is going on?** Urination is a sign of stress and is often associated with fear. It could be that your puppy is overwhelmed by your husband's size, voice, or any number of factors, and/or perhaps your puppy needs more time bonding with your husband. Most pups as they spend time with family members become much more comfortable and confident. Regardless, do not punish or yell at the puppy for nervous/ fear "leaking." This will only make the situation worse. A soft touch, pats, and more time together will help.

6 **What can I do to stop my dog from pushing his way out the front door and running?** Teach him a rock-solid *down-stay* or *sit-stay*. Attach a leash to your dog's collar and put him in a *stay* (either *down* or *sit*) at the front door. Step on his leash for safety. Reach for the doorknob and step back. Reward him for no movement. Give him the *stay* command again. Reach for the doorknob and turn it. Step back and reward him for no movement. Continue progressing until you can open and shut the door. Continue practicing with the leash at the front door.

7 **Why does my GSP steal the paper-towel roll and then growl when I try to take it away?** This is most likely resource guarding. Often a dog will pick one object, as *the* item he wants to have to himself. To prevent this situation from escalating, do the following:

a. Teach the *Out* command: Take an item that isn't highly valued and offer a treat as a swap. Say *"Out!"* as the dog drops the toy. Practice with different things, but make sure the swap is always irresistible.

b. Do not allow your GSP to have access to his high-value item.

c. Teach your children *never* to pull something out of the dog's mouth.

d. Never endanger yourself. If your GSP has an item and the swap isn't working, loop a leash around his head like a lasso, tighten

it up, and say, "Let's go!" and start walking briskly. Walk right out the front door and just keep walking. Give obedience commands, *sit, down, come,* and keep walking. Eventually, he will drop the item. You can go back and get it later. Have him perform some more obedience exercises and now reward him.

8 **How can I stop my GSP from digging?** Make sure he is getting enough exercise. GSPs will often dig if they are bored or have pent-up energy. If the digging is in one section of the yard, keep him out of this area with additional fencing.

9 **Why is my GSP eating the television remotes?** The height of a pup's teething begins as he loses his milk teeth and the adult teeth emerge, between four and five months of age. Provide lots of appropriate chewing items made for heavy chewers. And keep the remotes and all other potential chew items in drawers and locked behind cabinets.

10 **My GSP is counter-surfing. How do I train him not to?** He will smell anything and everything—and he's athletic enough to jump up on the counter and not make a noise. So how do you stop a counter surfer? If you must leave food on the counter and you aren't in the kitchen to supervise the dog, crate him. He's a GSP. Food is his reward. 'Nuff said.

Leash Training

1 Clip on your GSP's leash and start walking.

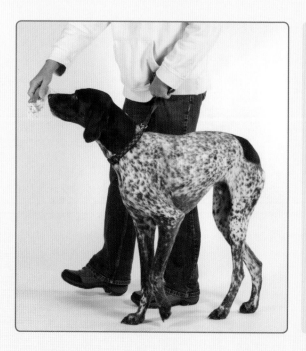

2 Keep a toy in your right hand and make sure he sees it as you're walking.

3 Stop frequently to allow him to play with the toy.

4 Reward him with praise!

The Sit Command

1 Hold your GSP's collar gently.

2 Hold a treat in your closed hand (fingers closed around the treat and the back of your hand toward the dog's nose).

3 Slowly move the treat toward your dog's ears, and he should begin to fold into a *sit*.

4 As he finishes the *sit*, say, "*Sit!*" Reward your pup with the treat.

The Stay Command

1 Put your GSP in a *sit*, and say, *"Stay!"* as you give him the stay hand signal.

2 Take a half step to the right, keeping your left foot in place.

3 Immediately step back to your dog.

4 Reward him!

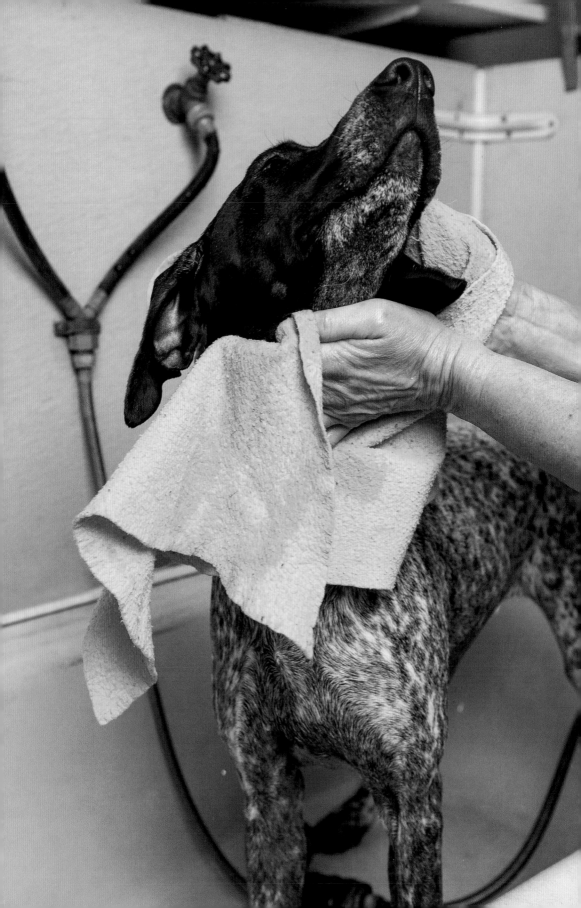

Chapter Eight

Grooming

When it comes to grooming, owners of German Shorthaired Pointers are typically very thankful. A GSP coat is short and easy to maintain. Although pendulous, the ears typically don't have as many problems as other breeds (although they should be kept clean). In short, with the shorthair no difficult grooming is involved.

How to Clip Nails

Who likes their nails trimmed, raise your paw! (Note the lack of response from GSPs present.) Although not particularly enjoyable, nail trimming is necessary. The GSP is an active dog, and nails that are too long can break, split, or even tear, making activity difficult or painful. If the nails are too long, the dog will rock his weight back on his paws so there is less pressure on the nails, which causes problems with movement and can flatten the foot.

Dogs don't particularly like their paws being held, and they definitely do not like them squeezed, although holding a clipper in your other hand seems to accentuate this dislike. The more you practice trimming nails while your dog is a puppy and make it a positive experience, the better your dog will behave when he is full grown.

Helpful Hints

What's Too Long?
You should not hear a noise from your dog's nails when he walks on a hard surface. If you do hear a click-click-click, the nails are too long.

Practice Makes Perfect
The less you linger and belabor the trimming process, the less stressed your GSP will be. If you can cut your GSP's nails swiftly and accurately, you will minimize your dog's chances of getting "wiggly" while his nails are being trimmed. Don't, however, go so fast that you make a lot of mistakes and begin to quick your dog's toenails.

To accomplish this, it helps to get as much practice time as possible. One of the ways you can do this is to practice nail trimming without actually trimming the nail, including holding the clipper against the nail. The earlier

Breed Truths

Dewclaws

Dewclaws are the fifth toe that is found on the inside of a dog's pasterns on his front legs. If you look at your puppy's legs, you probably won't find a dewclaw, because these are usually removed by the veterinarian when the puppy is just a few days old—at the same time the tail is docked. In the field, the presence of dewclaws is an increased risk to the dog, because this additional toe is in a prime location to become caught, torn, and broken in rough undergrowth. Not all breeders remove dewclaws, however. If your pup or adult has dewclaws, be vigilant in keeping the nail on this additional toe as short as possible. This will help protect against getting the nail caught while the dog is in the field.

you start this with your GSP, the better. These practice sessions are also a great way to heap praise and love on your GSP.

With enough practice of this kind, your GSP will learn to be well behaved while his paws are being handled, and will look forward to his love and treats, too. Don't fuss if you "quick" a nail; act as if it's "nothing." If you can keep moving on and continue clipping the rest of the nails, do so. But if you need to, take care of the quicked nail first.

Depending on how fast your GSP's nails grow, you may have to trim them every few weeks. If you are going to show your GSP in conformation classes, you will be expected to have your dog's nails very short and polished. (This will require more frequent trimming.) In field work, the nails should be a healthy, functioning length but don't need to be particularly short.

What do you do when you can't see the quick? This can be a problem with GSPs, as many of them have some, or all, black nails, and you can't see where the quick ends. (Clear nails enable you to easily see the pink quick through the nail.) If you turn the paw over, you will see an oval-shaped structure at the bottom of the nail. This oval shows you where the quick is. Cut just past it, to avoid cutting into the quick.

Toenail-Clipping Tools

There are several options for trimming nails, as listed below.

The "guillotine" clipper: This clipper has a place to put the nail through and "hold" it while the blade slides along a track and slices it off.

The "scissors" clipper: This clipper has two blades that close together like scissors blades. Often there is a "guard" that can be used to keep from cutting too much nail at one time.

The grinder: Although there are dedicated electric or battery-powered grinders for pet toenail trimming, most professionals just use a Dremel tool with a fine grind tip. Grinding has the benefit of being able to smooth and polish, in addition to allowing you to avoid quicking the nail. (You will start to see the pink before you actually quick it.) However, you have to be careful not to give your dog a "hot paw"—because these can really heat up if you aren't careful. Also, your dog will have to get used to the sound, smell,

FYI: Ways to Stop Bleeding Quickly!

If you quick your dog, there are several options. You can dip the nail into a powdered product such as Quik Stop, which will clot the flow of blood. You can use a styptic pencil on the quicked nail. You can also apply pressure with a paper towel until the bleeding has stopped. After you've stopped the bleeding, don't let your GSP run around too soon, as the clot needs to set a little while so it doesn't dislodge. This would be a good time to give him a yummy chew and allow him some quiet time in his crate.

and overall grinding sensation—some dogs really worry and resist this tool's use at first. Use the same strategies as with acclimating to a toenail clipper and work without grinding, rewarding for nonwiggly behavior and easing your shorthair into the grinding routine.

All About Teeth

Most people are very aware of human dental health but don't think about keeping their dog's teeth clean and free of decay. Just like people, however, dogs will have dental decay. The American Veterinary Dental Society says that 80 percent of dogs show dental disease by the age of three. GSPs tend to have healthier teeth than some of the more problematic toy breeds, but they are by no means immune.

How do you keep your GSP's teeth clean and healthy? First, don't use toothpaste meant for humans, because there are chemicals in it that would be harmful to your dog if he were to swallow them. (As smart as the shorthair is, he has not figured out how to spit out toothpaste.) Instead, use canine toothpaste with delectable doggie flavors, such as chicken or beef.

If you start your puppy with a toothbrush, he is more than likely going to gnaw and chew it, and not much brushing will get done. With a pup, use a finger

Helpful Hints

Some breeders swear by cutting the nail with a "guillotine" or vertical (up and down) cutting clippers. Some clippers have a scissors motion that lends itself to sideways cutting. Some breeders, however, think that cutting sideways causes discomfort in large dog nails but the "guillotine" style of cutting does not. If you would like to try this, and have a scissors-style nail cutter, you can hold it sideways so it is still cutting "up and down." Key, however, is that whatever style clippers you use, (1) they are the appropriate size for the dog, and (2) they are well made and very, very sharp. Dull blades of any type of clipper will crumble and splinter a nail as opposed to cutting it cleanly.

brush, which is made of rubber, and knobby. Be aware that puppy teeth are very sharp. When sticking your finger into his mouth, you may wonder if you're actually trying to brush the teeth of a great white shark.

Don't try to do too much the very first time you brush your puppy's teeth. Shoot for a quick rub or two and follow this with lots of praise. As your puppy gets used to it, you can add more of a brushing motion, especially at the place where he will build up the most plaque (where teeth and gums meet). Eventually you will be able to use a brush, but that's up to you.

When you brush, keep an eye out for problems. Look for anything different that could be a cavity or other problem, as well as broken or split teeth. (Be careful what you let your GSP chew—ask your veterinarian if you are in doubt about whether something is good or bad for your dog's teeth.) If you notice something amiss, see your veterinarian. Your veterinarian will also be able to advise you about things such as canine mouthwashes, gels, and foods that help your dog's dental health.

Just as you visit your dentist for routine cleaning even though you brush and floss every day (because your daily brushing routine will not completely prevent plaque buildup), so, too, will your dog need to visit the veterinarian for an annual cleaning. Veterinary cleanings are not inexpensive because they require that the dog be under light anesthesia during the process. The cleaner you keep your dog's teeth, however, the less expensive this visit to the veterinarian's office will be and the less time your dog will spend under anesthesia. An additional benefit of this annual cleaning is the application of a sealant to your dog's teeth, which helps retard the growth of plaque and tartar.

FYI: Oral Treats, Chews, Gels, and More That Work

Many products claim to have tartar- and plaque-removing capabilities. To ensure that the products you are buying are effective in retarding plaque and tartar, look for the "accepted" seal of approval by the Veterinary Oral Health Council (VOHC). The VOHC's list of products can be accessed at *www.vohc.org/ accepted_products.htm*. Products include treats, chews, gels, oral sprays, water additives, and foods. (Note: Dental foods are effective only if the dog chews his food.) In addition to brushing a dog's teeth (not in place of!) you might also consider the following helpful products, approved by the VOHC as being effective, of course.

- Anti-plaque water additive: Products vary, but roughly 1 tablespoon and 1 teaspoon are added to 1 gallon (3.8 L) of water; dog is "served" water as mixed.
- Anti-plaque gel: A thin layer of gel is applied to the gum line nightly after meals.
- Anti-plaque oral spray: The product is sprayed at the gum line nightly after meals.

Brushing

German Shorthaired Pointers naturally produce oil in their coats. Some coats are very soft and very short, and some are a tad longer and a bit coarser in texture. All GSP coats repel cockleburs, and anything that would "stick" to a typical dog's coat tends to be repelled by the shorthair's coat, in part because of this oil.

Very little is needed to maintain a GSP coat. Any basic, soft-bristle brush will do. You don't need a "hounds glove" with little needles, rakes, combs, or anything else. Find a brush that your GSP likes and brush him every few days, or as needed. Regular brushing is not needed to control mats as there is no long hair involved; however, regular brushing is good for dogs of all ages because it helps to spread the natural coat oils and stimulates the skin. It's also a bonding moment for many dogs and owners.

Helpful Hints

Using a rubber hand glove with knobs or a Zoom-Groom rubber brush while bathing can help you get past the shorthair's natural oils and give the skin a really good, deep massage.

With this said, GSPs do shed, most heavily in the spring and fall; however, in temperate climates you may find that your dog sheds moderately

SHOPPING LIST

Grooming Tools (It's a "Short"-Haired List!)

1. Nail clippers or grinder (or both)
2. Brush
3. Scissors (if you're going to trim whiskers for the show ring; otherwise, leave them alone)
4. Doggie shampoo (for the occasional bath)
5. Do not put bows on a GSP; they will be embarrassed and hate you for life. (Well, maybe not, but these are hunting dogs and deserve some respect.)

year-round. If you keep your GSP brushed, most coat shed will wind up in your brush and not on your furniture.

Bathing and Drying

You have the bathtub cleared out, the water warmed up, shampoo at the ready, and towels stacked for drying. As you start running water over your shorthair's coat, you realize that he's not getting wet. The water is running off the coat as though you had lacquered it with a repellant. What you are seeing is why GSP coats are so effective at not picking up cockleburs in the field—these are your shorthair's natural oils at work. Some GSPs have less oil in their coat and do get "wet" eventually, but don't be surprised if you have to apply shampoo and massage it in to break through this natural barrier.

Once you've massaged your shampoo in (don't forget the belly and inside the legs), you will see the coat get "wet" when you rinse the shampoo back out. Don't worry. The oils will return on their own. It's okay, too, if you have to bathe your GSP frequently to keep him clean and smelling nice, as he will get into things in the field.

When you bathe your GSP, avoid getting shampoo in his eyes and ears. Use a rubber brush to help remove difficult and caked-on dirt. Make sure to rinse thoroughly and then rinse thoroughly again. Your dog will itch and scratch if you don't wash out the shampoo thoroughly. The

Helpful Hints

If you have a self-service dog wash in your area, take advantage of the easy access to the washing tubs, warm water, unlimited shampoos and conditioners, clean towels, and warm blow dryers. It may be a bit of a "spa" for the shorthair, but it makes cleaning up your bathroom much easier—because there's not a dog in your tub.

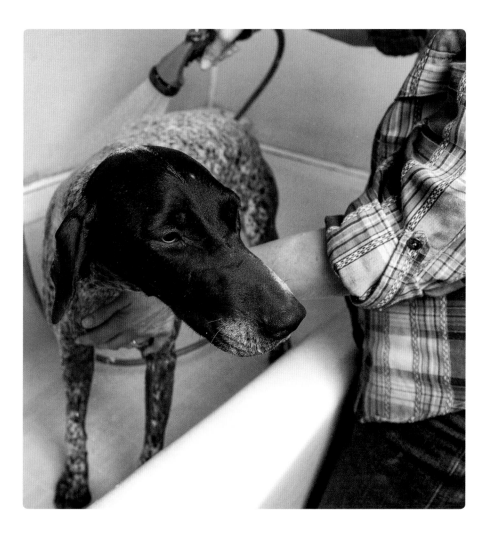

water should be clear, with no suds or bubbles. Make sure your dog's paws are free of residual shampoo.

Drying is easily accomplished through a combination of letting your dog shake, using your hands to "squeegee" off extra water, and finally using towels to dry him off. If the ears are wet, make sure they are dried, too. (See "Ear Maintenance," page 146.) If you have bathed him inside the house, make sure the door to the bathroom is shut completely when he gets out of the tub, or he will fly out of the bath area and make a beeline for beds and pieces of furniture that you don't want a wet dog on, because of course, that is what he thinks he should dry himself on.

Though the coat will dry quickly, you can also use a blow dryer on a "warm" setting (not "hot") and dry the dog's coat, paying particular attention to drying under the flaps of the ears. Holding the dryer a couple of feet from the ear canals can help to rid them of any excess water.

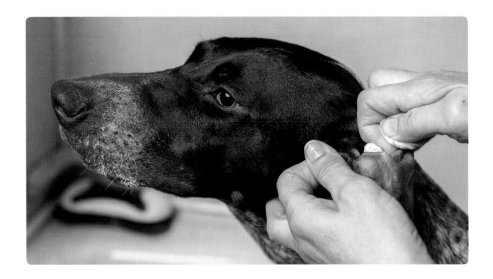

Breed Needs

Warning Signs for "EAR"-ly Detection of Infections

1. Do the ears smell really bad? They shouldn't, and if they do, this is a warning sign of an ear infection.
2. Is there any redness, inflammation, blood, and/or excessive wax or dark, waxy secretions? There shouldn't be, and if there is, you will want to take your dog to the veterinarian.
3. Is there head shaking, scratching, holding the head at an odd angle, or increased sensitivity to touch? Have your veterinarian examine your GSP. Ear infections can cause permanent, lasting damage.

Ear Maintenance

The dog's ear canal is structured differently from a human's ear canal and is not a straight tube to the eardrum. The dog's ear has a bend that can sometimes make deep cleaning of an ear more difficult, particularly on a dog that is out in the field and has greater potential to come in contact with contaminated water and vegetation, or worse yet, manage to get something lodged in its ear canal.

For regular ear maintenance (after bathing, swimming, and being in the field), you should use a cleansing/drying antiseptic ear wash (such as OtiRinse). Put several drops in the dog's ear and massage the ear at the base. (Don't let him shake his head yet!) The massaging will help to loosen up wax and crust that has accumulated in the dog's ear. After massaging for 10–20 seconds, place a cotton ball in the opening of his ear, place your thumb on the cotton ball, and massage it. The cotton ball will wick up the broken-up debris in the dog's ear. Replace with another cotton ball until the ball is clean.

Use a cotton swab dipped in the cleansing/drying ear wash and clean out the deep folds in the dog's ear. Wipe with a dry cotton ball and then let your dog shake his head. Repeat with the other ear. If you find that your shorthair is producing copious amounts of a darker, brown waxy substance, a more determined cleaning may be necessary, but only after a trip to the veterinarian to ensure that the dog does not have a foreign body lodged in his ear or a potential ear infection. Have your veterinarian show you how to clean your dog's ear canals thoroughly and safely.

Helpful Hints

Allergies can be a source of chronic ear infections and the production of copious amounts of wax and discharge.

The Eyes Have It

A normal eye will not have any discharge or film. A GSP should have a clear, dark, and expressive eye. Just like a person, a GSP can have a little bit of occasional residue in his eyes that is easy to wipe clean. If you find that your dog's eyes are producing a greenish discharge, he may have conjunctivitis or another type of eye infection. See your veterinarian immediately.

When it comes to your shorthair's eyes, anything other than the normal should be examined more closely. Reddened whites, inflammation, excessive tears, or any other type of discharge could be caused by an injury or by a more serious eye condition. If your dog's eyes are itchy or inflamed, he will try to scratch them or rub them, which risks injury to the eye. You will want your veterinarian to be sure your GSP doesn't have an injury, a malformed eyelash, an infection, or some other kind of disease that is causing these problems.

Chapter Nine

The Senior German Shorthaired Pointer

T he quality of your aging shorthair's life will be greatly dependent on your continued loving and diligent care. Understanding the potential difficulties and discomforts that can accompany the normal aging process can go far in your ability to successfully keep him comfortable and healthy.

Enriching an Older Dog's Life

The fact that your GSP has reached his senior years might sneak up on you. The shorthair that you used to jog five miles with every day may now be content to snooze on the couch or at your feet most of the day. His muzzle, which was once a rich, dark liver, may have grizzled with gray.

Just because the GSP has finally settled down and become a "hearth" dog does not mean that this inactivity is good for him! Or that he wouldn't enjoy some of the same activities he so loved when he was a younger dog. In fact, enriching your shorthair's life physically, mentally, and emotionally in his senior and geriatric years is believed to help immensely with improving his quality of life.

Exercise As an active breed, the GSP is perhaps even more likely to suffer from arthritis by his senior years than less active breeds. (See "Arthritis," page 154.) Gentle exercise will not only help keep arthritic joints moving but also help to increase your shorthair's circulation, and benefit his heart and lungs. Obesity can be an issue in older dogs, including the GSP, and gentle exercise can help keep the "less food + more exercise = weight loss" equation balanced.

New People and Places Even if your GSP isn't very mobile, it's still important to take him places and to occasionally meet new people. Socialization never stops, and continually taking an older, adult dog out of the house for car rides and short trips to parks (the same one he used to run to when he was young) helps keep him from becoming territorial of his home. It's also a great way to stimulate him mentally with lots of scents, sounds, and sights.

Mental Tasks No dog is too old to learn something new if it's within his physical abilities. All that time you spent training him in basic skills as a puppy through adulthood is missed! Training not only stimulates your GSP mentally but provides your shorthair with perhaps the most valuable commodity of all—time with you.

Hands On Obviously you don't have to worry about a GSP's coat becoming matted, but daily brushing with a soft-bristle brush provides appreciated bonding time with you, as well as helps to spread the dog's natural coat oils (which keep the aging dog's skin softer) and stimulates the skin.

Appreciation To have a GSP live into his senior and geriatric years is not uncommon; these dogs can be very healthy. No one, however, knows how long even the healthiest of dogs will live. Never take a day for granted, and appreciate every moment you are given with this wonderful family member.

Breed Truths

When Is the GSP a Senior?

Current age analogies are based primarily on a breed's weight. With an average weight of 55 to 70 pounds (25–32 kg), the GSP would be considered a "senior" from six to nine years of age and a "geriatric" from ten years on. The average life span of a GSP is currently 10 to 12 years.

Veterinary Care for Seniors

Once your GSP reaches his senior years, your veterinarian will likely

BE PREPARED! Establishing What's Normal Now

The following tests are typically given when a dog reaches his senior years and serve as a baseline when your GSP becomes ill, enabling your veterinarian to determine what is abnormal more quickly.

Test	What It Is	What Abnormal Results Could Indicate
Complete Blood Cell Count (CBC)	A count of the numbers of white and red blood cells	Depending on whether the red or the white cell counts are abnormal, possible issues could be anemia, infection, or disease.
Blood Chemistry Profile	A test that looks for the presence of chloride, cholesterol, electrolytes; liver, pancreatic, muscle, and, perhaps, bone enzymes; glucose, proteins, potassium, etc., in the blood	If a value is outside the "normal" range for a specific component in the blood, it could be an early indicator of disease or, depending on which blood component is abnormal, a sign of decreased or compromised functioning of the thyroid, liver, kidneys, pancreas, muscles, or bone.
Urinalysis	A chemical analysis of the urine that records pH value, and looks for the presence of components that should not be present in urine	Depending on what is present (i.e., crystals, blood, proteins, etc.), the urinalysis could show signs of such problems as disease, infection, fever, or dehydration.

ask to have "baseline" tests performed on your dog. (See "Be Prepared! Establishing What's Normal Now," above.) These tests will include some blood work as well as a urinalysis. Basically, this sets up a baseline of what is normal for your dog, so that when he becomes ill, a new test will show variances.

In addition, your veterinarian will suggest that rather than annual exams, your senior dog come in for exams every six months. This is not an effort to make more money! Every year once he's of senior age, your GSP is aging the equivalent of five to six "human" years. Would you suggest that people in their 70s or 80s go to the doctor for a checkup only every five or six years? Probably not.

A lot can happen in a short time when a dog is of advanced age. The best news, however, is that many diseases and conditions can be halted if caught early enough. If the disease can't be cured, it often can be treated to slow its progression. Even if the latter isn't possible, it is always possible to make choices that directly affect the comfort and quality of life of your GSP.

Changes to Watch For

Oftentimes you may not notice any sudden changes in your GSP's overall condition as he ages, but it is important to watch for more gradual changes that require special attention or could indicate the presence of disease.

Skin Circulation in older dogs may not be what it used to be, and you may notice a drier coat and/or more sensitive skin. Gentle brushing can help stimulate circulation and will help spread natural coat oils. Older GSPs with hypothyroidism (see page 102) may start to show changes in their skin and hair loss as they approach their senior years, too.

Nails Be careful with clipping the senior's nails; not only can they be more brittle (and crumble with less sharp clippers), but if the GSP has arthritis, holding his paw up to clip them may be painful to his joints.

Teeth If your senior GSP is suddenly refusing to retrieve, or carry a dumbbell, or simply not eating with his normal gusto, have your veterinarian check his teeth immediately! Older dogs commonly have tooth decay, broken teeth, and other very painful conditions in their mouths.

Changes in Appetite This is typically a sign of illness (or a tooth problem!). If your veterinarian has ruled these issues out, consider making his food more palatable.

Stools Blood and/or excessive mucus in the stools means an immediate trip to the veterinarian, as does diarrhea. If your dog's stools are more copious, it could be that he is not metabolizing his food as well as he used to when he was younger. Talk to your veterinarian about options for senior diets, which tend to be packed with more nutrients that are more highly digestible.

Managing Incontinence

Female dogs that have been spayed are at greater risk of developing incontinence at some point in their life, usually as they age. If your GSP has been immaculate all her life and then begins to "leak" (this is different from having an accident), she may be having issues with incontinence.

First, make sure your veterinarian has ruled out other possible causes for pooling urine, such as urinary tract infections, diabetes, kidney disease, and hypothyroidism, which all can cause an increase in drinking and an urgent need to urinate. If your veterinarian determines your GSP is incontinent, there are several things you can do to manage the situation, including managing her weight (lessens pressure on the bladder), exercise (helps to tone supporting muscles), picking up water 30 minutes before bedtime, and allowing for voiding the bladder before all periods of sleep throughout the day and night.

Medical intervention is also possible. Medications are available that are inexpensive, effective, and considered very safe for long-term use with few side effects. Additionally, in cases in which medication does not work, a procedure is available in which collagen injections are used to narrow the urinary sphincter.

Working with Cognitive Dysfunction Syndrome (CDS)

If your GSP reaches geriatric age (beginning at ten), he is at increased risk of developing Cognitive Dysfunction Syndrome (CDS). Symptoms include disorientation, variances in social behaviors (sudden fearfulness, aggression, odd behaviors around other dogs), interrupted sleep cycle, and loss of housetraining.

Currently there is no cure for CDS; however, research indicates that a combination of environmental enrichment (see "Enriching an Older Dog's Life," page 149) and a special diet provides the greatest improvement in a dog's cognitive abilities. The diet that has shown promise in slowing CDS was developed by Hill's Pet Nutrition (Canine b/d®). Additionally, a medication that has been shown effective in treating CDS is L-Deprenyl (Anipryl).

HOME BASICS
What You Can Do to Ease Arthritic Pain

With the addition of a few gentle care basics and some simple, inexpensive changes to your home, you can create a much friendlier environment for your aging, arthritic GSP.

Exercise: Swimming is ideal; however, a nice, gentle daily walk that's not too long will help keep your GSP's joints from getting too stiff.

Diet: If your GSP is overweight, work on having him reduce, because every pound counts on those joints.

Footing: If you have wood and/or tile floors, place nonslip rugs and runners throughout major travel areas. Make sure "landing" areas at the bottom of steps also have a nonslip surface.

Bedding: Provide orthopedic bedding, cooling gel pads, and/or thick memory-foam bedding for your GSP. These will be supportive and help spread pressure points.

Elevate bowls: If your GSP eats standing up, it can become very difficult for him to eat out of a bowl off the floor. If he doesn't automatically lie down when he eats, consider feeding him out of raised bowls.

Ramps: If it's difficult for you to lift your GSP into the car, consider purchasing a dog ramp that can make it possible for him to continue going on car rides as usual.

Arthritis

The GSP is not a heavy dog; however, he is a very active dog. Active dogs put more wear and tear on their joints than those that are less active. When the cartilage wears down in a dog's joints (whether that's from being a giant breed with joints forced to bear more weight, an overweight toy breed, or an athletic, active GSP), the dog loses his natural cushioning. As the bones become closer together or even touch, the joint becomes painful and inflamed, and can become painfully debilitating.

Your GSP, as a model of stoicism, isn't likely to exhibit much sign of pain when arthritis is in its early stages. As the arthritis becomes more serious, and as the cartilage wears down to a thin pad, you are likely to see more signs of arthritic pain: slow to rise from lying down, a slight limp until the dog "warms" up, heat in the joint or slight swelling, or a leg that splays when the dog rounds the corner or tries to stand up quickly (resulting in a "froggie-dog" position that puppies can do easily but older dogs, not so much).

In addition to several adaptive home measures that can make your GSP's life immediately more comfortable (see "Home Basics: What You Can Do to Ease Arthritic Pain," above), there are several nutritional and medical options that can help ease your GSP's arthritic symptoms. These options include joint supplements, NSAIDs, pain medications, and surgical options.

Joint Supplements Supplements, such as glucosamine, chondroitin sulfate, and MSM (Methylsulfonylmethane), have been recommended for some time to help ease the symptoms of arthritis in dogs. Often, senior foods will contain these joint supplements as an added benefit. If your GSP isn't receiving joint supplements, talk to your veterinarian about current dosage and product recommendations. Keep in mind that joint supplements need to be taken daily and that it may take as much as four to six weeks to see benefits.

NSAIDs Nonsteroidal anti-inflammatory drugs (NSAIDs) don't work for every dog, and some carry the potential for serious side effects, but when they do work for a dog, the results can be amazing. (You may not have realized how much your GSP's pain had slowed him down until he doesn't feel the pain!) NSAIDs are available through prescription only.

Pain Medications In some instances, a GSP may not be able to tolerate long-term use of NSAIDs, or the NSAIDs may not provide him with enough

Lipomas, Calluses, and Warts

As your GSP ages, you may find that he develops some changes in and under his skin. At first appearance, you should always have skin changes examined by your veterinarian to rule out anything more serious; however, the following conditions are considered relatively benign and are not uncommon in elderly GSPs.

Lipomas This is a fatty tumor that is found under the skin. It is usually (but not always) softer and moves easily under the skin. It is a benign tumor that is diagnosed with a needle aspiration. Lipomas are not removed as a general rule unless they are in a location that makes it uncomfortable for the dog (such as under an armpit, restricting movement, or on the dog's chest, preventing the dog from lying down comfortably). Since mast cell tumors in their early stages can be mistaken for lipomas, it is important to have each new "lump" checked by your veterinarian.

Calluses Dogs that like to lie on hard surfaces (think "tile floor in summer") will often develop thick, gray, hairless calluses on pressure points, such as the elbows and hocks. These calluses generally do not present any problems unless they are damaged somehow, and then as with any wound, the area could become infected. To prevent these calluses from forming (or from getting any larger and more unsightly) offer the elderly GSP a cooling water- or gel-filled pad in the summer—unless he's a shredder even in old age.

Warts Many older GSPs may develop what appears to be a wart. True warts are the result of the papillomavirus, and though not attractive, they are typically not a health risk, nor are they typically removed. Warts can be a sign of the GSP being immunocompromised and can (rarely) transform to squamous cell carcinoma. Other growths that can appear to be a wart but are not include skin adnexal tumors, especially sebaceous gland adenomata, and benign and malignant basal cell tumors. If your GSP has what appears to be a wart, have your veterinarian confirm this.

pain relief. In these cases, your veterinarian may prescribe a painkiller. This won't reduce inflammation, but it will reduce his pain.

Surgical Options Is surgery a viable option for the geriatric GSP with severe arthritis? It depends on the amount of pain your GSP is in, the joint affected, your GSP's overall health, your ability to care for your GSP during his recovery, and your financial capacity to pay for a joint-replacement operation ($3,500 or more). Obviously, you would not want to put an aging GSP through a major surgery if the outcome was not anticipated to be good. This is the time to have a serious discussion with your veterinarian, who can counsel you about the benefits versus the risks of surgery.

Are You on the Same Page?

Caring for a chronically ill, cherished pet is never easy. It can be time-consuming, exhausting work, and emotionally and physically draining. When it comes to making hard decisions, it helps to work with a veterinarian who shares your desire to maintain the highest quality of life for your GSP and is in agreement about when you have to draw the line in potentially expensive care and treatments.

Ultimately, no one knows your GSP as well as you do. If you are in an end-of-life care situation, and your veterinarian tells you, "You will know when it's time. He will tell you," trust yourself. Your GSP will tell you. Open your heart and listen, and be thankful for all the wonderful, amazing memories he has given you.

Chapter Ten

For German Shorthairs Especially

One of the most satisfying undertakings for a GSP owner is working a dog in an activity for which he has been bred to excel. There is an intense bond that develops between a dog and owner, and sharing this activity with your dog will create moments that are truly unforgettable.

Doing What Comes Naturally . . . Which Is Everything

German Shorthaired Pointers were bred to do it all. The wealthy could afford to have individual dogs for pointing, retrieving in water, and trailing game, but the everyday hunter might be able to afford and keep only one dog. Thus, the Germans developed a "versatile" breed that could point upland bird, trail game, retrieve game over land and water, protect the home, and chase away vermin.

Note that although the GSP can do all these things well, he generally cannot do it as well as a breed that was specifically bred for one activity. For instance, the best English Pointers typically run farther and faster than a GSP (although they might fly past birds that the GSP won't miss). A retrieving breed, such as a Labrador Retriever, can "break ice" and retrieve in bitterly cold waters that a GSP is not truly equipped to handle as well. But if you have ever seen an English Pointer trying to swim, or a Lab "point" a bird, you will appreciate the German Shorthaired Pointer's ability to handle everything you throw at him with aplomb and style.

GSPs have an excellent nose. It is not unusual for them to lock on point from 25 yards to 50 yards (7.5–15 m) away from a solitary quail in a driving rain. (This is quite a feat, but hunters will testify to amazing feats such as this and more.) Good field GSPs instinctively hunt the "edges," such as hedgerows and edges of woods where wild game birds are most likely to be. They will "quarter" (move back and forth in a zigzag pattern) across the wind, so they do not "miss" any game scent.

Some GSPs are close working, and prefer not to work ahead of the hunter for more than 75 yards (22.5 m). These dogs make excellent foot-hunting companions. Other GSPs have a great deal of "run" and will range out up to a half mile or mile away at full speed. These dogs tend to be competitive field-trial dogs, and are often handled off horseback.

Virtually every GSP has some pointing instinct. The classic form is with the tail held at about a 45-degree angle to the topline. Contrary to what a lot of people think, a point does not necessarily mean that one front paw is held up in the air. In fact, a point is basically a stalk that is "frozen" in time. It is just as common to have all four feet on the ground as it is to have one front foot in the air.

In competitive field trials, the most desirable pointing form is rock solid, without a quiver, head held either high or with an intense gaze at the game; a "high" tail, one that is closer to vertical from the topline, is generally preferred.

GSPs generally make good retrievers. However, they need to be trained to reinforce their natural retrieving instinct. Most have no qualms about leaping into the water, and they are powerful swimmers with their naturally webbed feet.

Although maybe not as fast as an English Pointer, GSPs can run and hunt for hours on end if they are conditioned properly. Most hunters like to rest them every 30 minutes to an hour, and care should be taken not to overdo it early in the hunting season if your GSP has been lazing about the house all summer.

Breed Truths

Despite their apparent love of cold, muddy water when going after a downed bird, they will usually either glare at you or look heartbroken when you give them a bath with nice, warm water. Go figure.

Beginning Strategies for Future Hunters

You're watching your little liver-and-white bundle of GSP joy and you start to daydream . . . "I wonder if he could hunt . . ." Here are some activities you can work on with your dog to begin building that bond and developing your dream hunting companion.

Basic Obedience

GSPs have a tendency to think they know best. It is helpful to begin some training early on. For hunting purposes, the first command most people teach is the *come* command (see *Come*, page 124).

Most field-trial trainers and hunt trainers do not teach *sit* or *down* commands. Why? Because when a dog is on point, he is under an enormous amount of mental pressure. Every instinct he has is telling him to break point and run in and get that bird. But as he progresses in his training, he learns he has to wait—even while his handler walks past him to get to that bird first and kick it up into the air. Even more pressure! It is considered very bad form to *sit* or *lie down* when on point. And, if previously trained to do so, there is a tendency for a dog under pressure to do just that.

Now, if your interest is obedience competition, clearly the above does not apply. There are some who have successfully trained for both obedience and field work. However, it is easier to train for field work first, and when that is solid, start in competitive obedience.

Retrieve

Although GSPs have a retrieve instinct, it is not as developed as in a dedicated retriever. Retrieves must be trained—you cannot rely on instinct alone. However, most trainers do not begin retrieve training (on birds) until well after general hunting training has begun. The enthusiasm for finding the birds is always developed first. Having said that, learning to retrieve a "dummy" and making it fun can be done early on. (See "The Foundations of Fetch," page 165.)

Acclimate to Woods and Fields

GSPs typically love to run in woods and fields. Acclimation is not a problem, although a recall might be. Use a long line and practice your dog's recall command (see *Come,* page 124), ensuring that he succeeds.

An Introduction to Water

There are many different ways to do this. Some trainers like to take a very hot, tired dog after a long run, carry him into a lake or pond, and let him swim a few yards back to shore. Some GSPs dive into water without a second thought. Some need a reason to go in, like retrieving a dummy. Not all GSPs "love" the water, but they are almost all willing to go in and get the job done.

Avoiding Making a Dog Gun Shy

More people have ruined bird dogs by improperly introducing the sound of a gun being fired than any other training sin out there. Here is a way

Helpful Hints

If you are interested in competition or a particular aspect of hunting, it is important to determine the potential hunting style and drives of a puppy before making a purchase. Ask your breeder about the hunting habits of the parents, so that you have an idea of what your puppy's "style" may be, and be sure to communicate where your interests in hunting lie and your expectations for the GSP as a hunter.

to introduce the sound of a gun going off that is a surefire way (pun intended) to develop a confident gundog.

First, your GSP should be finding and, preferably, pointing birds. At a young age, the point will be fleeting before the dog takes off running trying to "get" the bird. This is just fine. In fact, you want to see that enthusiasm. You want your GSP to be running like a madman after that pigeon that just took off, focused solely on grabbing some piece of that bird in its jaws, when you fire off the first round.

Second, don't start with a 12-gauge loaded with some magnum round. That first shot should be as soft as you can make it. Use a starter pistol or a small-gauge shotgun. And you absolutely wait until the dog is in full flight chasing that bird. Fire your pistol pointing away from the dog and wait until he has got some distance on you. He will barely hear the gun. And he will hear it doing something that is far more exciting. Within a few repetitions, he will associate his chasing after those game birds with the gun. And he will never be afraid of one going off, because that now means to him, "There are birds here!"

Eventually, your GSP should start going bananas with joy when you take a shotgun down and hold it, figuring the two of you are going to go hunting. This is what you want.

Working with Horses

GSPs who are intent on hunting might look at a horse with curiosity the first time they see one. They might even be a bit leery, but once they're off and running, they typically don't give a horse a second thought. When he is young, though, it is advisable not to ride up close to your dog on point. Dismount, let someone hold your horse, and walk the rest of the way.

The Foundations of Fetch

With your pup on a line, throw a bumper, a ball, or something you've seen him want to pick up, down a carpeted hallway in your home, or outside. Don't throw it too far. Your pup will run after it and pick it up. He may or may not start running back to you with it, because this is his prize!

Encourage him to head your way (the line will keep him from running off). You can start running away from him, and he will instinctively chase after you. Don't grab his "prize" from him when he gets to you, or he will learn immediately not to retrieve to you. Instead, make a big fuss over him until he drops it or until you give him a food reward treat. (Almost all GSPs are food fanatics, and will drop anything—except a bird—for food.)

Make this a game and don't play too long. Your pup should want more when you stop.

Competitive and Noncompetitive Hunting Events

Water Tests (GSPCA)

The German Shorthaired Pointer Club of America offers titles for different levels of ability in the water. Novice Retrieving Dog, Retrieving Dog, and Retrieving Dog Excellent are titles now offered that test increasingly difficult retrieves on land and water.

Helpful Hints

Finding a Training Club

If you do not have any experience in field training, it is a great idea to join a local training club. The North American Versatile Hunting Dog Association has quite a few such clubs scattered throughout the country. Although you can learn from books and videos, nothing beats someone working with you and showing you how it's done.

You can also work with a professional trainer to learn these skills. (Do keep your eyes open, though. Some trainers are used to breeds that are much "harder" than a GSP, and use methods that are too harsh. Use the breeder as a resource to find a good trainer who truly understands GSPs.)

Novice Retrieving Dog (NRD): At the entry level, NRD, the dog must retrieve a dead bird in the water one time with a minimum swim distance of 20 yards (6 m), during which time a shot will be fired.

Pointing Breed Hunt Tests (AKC, UKC)

Open to all pointing breeds, these events test the dog's ability to find game, point, and retrieve to hand (in the higher levels). Higher standards and "manners" are expected as the dog progresses to higher levels.

Junior Hunter (JH): At the entry level for AKC hunt tests, the dog must show that he is "hunting," and must find birds and come to a point, although he is not required to hold the point.

Shoot to Retrieve (NSTRA)

This is a competition that is timed. Two dogs run with their handlers (a handler can either shoot alone or have a dedicated shooter with him). The dogs must point and hold point until the bird is in the air (holding until after the shot is not required). Points are awarded for the number of birds found, shot, and retrieved, in addition to "style."

Champion (CH): In this NSTRA Shoot to Retrieve competition, the dog must hunt with style, find and point birds, be steady to wing, and perform retrieves of each bird shot. There is no entry level, as this is an actual competition. Multiple wins are required to earn the title.

Field Trials (AKC and American Field)

Field trials also test the run and hunting ability of a dog, but typically do not involve shooting birds on course. (The American Field trials are open to GSPs, but typically are populated by pointers and setters, and always use blank guns.) Finalists for placement in AKC trials are often "called back" to demonstrate a retrieve of a bird.

Field Champion/Amateur Field Champion (FC/AFC): Dog must hunt with style, find and point birds, be steady to shot, and perform a retrieve of a downed bird. There is no entry level in AKC field trials, as this is actual competition. Multiple wins are required to earn the title.

Versatility Tests (NAVHDA)

These are not a competition, but a test of all of the GSP's abilities. Hunting, retrieving, water retrieving, trailing, obedience, and conformation are all tested. The tests become increasingly difficult at the higher levels.

Natural Ability (NA): This entry-level NAVHDA test comprises basic hunting/pointing ability, a willingness to go into the water, tracking the scent of game, and general obedience and basic cooperation. It is designed to measure potential more than performance.

National Bird Dog Club of America

This organization offers the National Bird Dog Challenge, which is fun for the competitors and can earn additional titles for their dogs.

Resources

Organizations

American Kennel Club (AKC)
5580 Centerview Drive
Raleigh, NC 27606-3390
(919) 233-9767
www.akc.org

Canadian Kennel Club
200 Ronson Drive, Suite 400
Etobicoke, Ontario, Canada
M9W 5Z9
(416) 675-5511
www.ckc.ca

Deutsch-Kurzhaar-Verband e. V.
www.deutsch-kurzhaar.de

The Kennel Club (United Kingdom)
1-5 Clarges Street
Piccadilly, London W1J 8AB
0844-463-3980
www.the-kennel-club.org.uk

Fédération Cynologique Internationale
FCI Office
Place Albert 1er, 13
B-6530 THUIN
Belgique
Tel.: ++32.71.59.12.38
www.fci.be

German Shorthaired Pointer Club of America
www.gspca.org

German Shorthaired Pointer Club of Canada
www.gspcanada.com

North American Deutsch Kurzhaar Club
www.nadkc.org

National German Shorthaired Pointer Rescue (an affiliate of the GSPCA)
www.rescue.gspca.org

United Kennel Club (UKC)
100 E. Kilgore Road
Kalamazoo, MI 49002-5584
(269) 343-9020
www.ukcdogs.com

Health Organizations

Canine Eye Registration Foundation (CERF)
Veterinary Medical DataBases—
VMDB / CERF
1717 Philo Road
P.O. Box 3007
Urbana, IL 61803-3007
(217) 693-4800
www.vmdb.org/cerf.html

Canine Health Information Center (CHIC)
2300 E. Nifong Boulevard
Columbia, MO 65201-3806
(573) 442-0418
www.caninehealthinfo.org

Orthopedic Foundation for Animals (OFA)
2300 E. Nifong Boulevard
Columbia, MO 65201-3806
(573) 442-0418
www.offa.org

University of Pennsylvania Hip Improvement Program (PennHip)
University of Pennsylvania School of Veterinary Medicine
3800 Spruce Street
Philadelphia, PA 19104
research.vet.upenn.edu

Activities/Behavior

Agility
American Kennel Club (AKC)
See listing under "Organizations."

Canine Performance Events. Inc. (CPE)
P.O. Box 805
South Lyon, MI 48178
www.k9cpe.com

North American Dog Agility Council (NADAC)
P.O. Box 1206
Colbert, OK 74733
www.nadac.com
info@nadac.com

United Kennel Club (UKC)
See listing under "Organizations."

United States Dog Agility Association (USDAA)
P.O. Box 850995
Richardson, TX 75085
(972) 487-2200
www.usdaa.com

Animal-Assisted Therapy
The Delta Society
875 124th Avenue NE, Suite 101
Bellevue, WA 98005-2531
(425) 679-5500
www.deltasociety.org
info@deltasociety.org

Therapy Dogs International, Inc.
88 Bartley Road
Flanders, NJ 07836
(973) 252-9800
www.tdi-dog.org
tdi@gti.net

R.E.A.D.® (Reading Education Assistance Program)
Intermountain Therapy Animals
P.O. Box 17201
Salt Lake City, UT 84117
(801) 272-3439
www.therapyanimals.org
info@therapyanimals.org

Behavior/Training
Animal Behavior Society
Indiana University
2611 E. 10th Street
Bloomington, IN 47408-2603
(812) 856-5541
www.animalbehaviorsociety.org

American College of Veterinary Behaviorists (ACVB)
A listing of all current diplomates from the ACVB is on the organization's web site at *www.dacvb.org.*

American Veterinary Medical Association
1931 N. Meacham Road, Suite 100
Schaumburg, IL 60173-4360
(800) 248-2862
www.avma.org
avmainfo@avma.org

Association of Pet Dog Trainers (APDT)
101 N. Main Street, Suite 610
Greenville, SC 29601
(800) PET-DOGS ([800] 738-3647)
www.apdt.com

International Association of Canine Professionals
P.O. Box 560156
Montverde, FL 34756-0156
(877) THE-IACP
www.canineprofessionals.com

National Association of Dog Obedience Instructors
P.O. Box 1439
Socorro, NM 87801
(505) 850-5957
www.nadoi.org

Canine Good Citizen
See "American Kennel Club" listing.

Conformation
See "American Kennel Club" listing.
See "United Kennel Club" listing.

Field Trials/Hunt Tests
See "American Kennel Club" listing.
See "GSPCA" listing.
See "North American Deutsch Kurzhaar Club."
See "United Kennel Club" listing.

National Shoot to Retrieve Association
203 N. Mill Street
Plainfield, IN 46168
(317) 839-4059
www.nstra.org

North American Gun Dog Association
17850 County Road 54
Burlington, CO 80807
(719) 342-0776
www.nagdog.com

**North American Versatile Hunting
Dog Association**
P.O. Box 520
Arlington Heights, IL 60006
(847) 253-6488
www.navhda.org

Flyball
**North American Flyball
Association**
1400 W. Devon Avenue, #512
Chicago, IL 60660
(800) 318-6312
www.flyball.org

**United Flyball League
International**
PMB 169
4132 S. Rainbow Boulevard
Las Vegas, NV 89103
(702) 527-UFLI (8354)
www.u-fli.com

Musical Freestyle
**World Canine Freestyle
Organization**
P.O. Box 350122
Brooklyn, NY 11235
(718) 332-8336
www.worldcaninefreestyle.org
wdfodogs@aol.com

Musical Dog Sport Association
9211 West Road, #143-104
Houston, TX 77064
www.musicaldogsport.org

Obedience
See "American Kennel Club" listing.
See "United Kennel Club" listing.

Rally
See "American Kennel Club" listing.
See "Association of Pet Dog
Trainers."

Search and Rescue
**National Association for Search
and Rescue, Inc.**
www.nasar.org

Tracking
See "American Kennel Club" listing.

Books

Activities
Agility: Leach, Laurie. *The Beginner's
Guide to Dog Agility.* Neptune, NJ:
TFH, 2006.
Animal-Assisted Therapy: Davis,
Kathy Diamond. *Therapy Dogs:
Training Your Dog to Reach
Others.* Wenatchee, WA: Dogwise
Publishing, 2002.
Canine Good Citizen: Volhard, Jack,
and Wendy Volhard. *The Canine
Good Citizen: Every Dog Can Be
One,* 2nd Edition. New York: John
Wiley & Sons, 1997.
Clicker Training: Pryor, Karen.
*Getting Started: Clicker Training for
Dogs,* 4th Edition. Waltham, MA:
Sunshine Books, 2005.
Conformation: Migliorini,
Mario, and Peter Green. *New
Secrets of Successful Show Dog
Handling.* Crawford, CO: Alpine
Publications, 2002.
Flyball: Olson, Lonnie. *Flyball
Racing: The Dog Sport for Everyone.*
New York: John Wiley & Sons,
1997.
Obedience: Donaldson, Jean. *Train
Your Dog Like a Pro.* New York:
Howell Book House, 2010.
Rally: Eldredge, Debra. *The Ultimate
Guide to Rally-O: Rules, Strategies,
and Skills for Successful Rally
Obedience Competition.* Neptune,
NJ: TFH, 2011.

Search and Rescue: American Rescue Dog Association. *Search and Rescue Dogs: Training the K-9 Hero,* 2nd Edition. New York: John Wiley & Sons, 2002.

Tracking: Krause, Carolyn. *Try Tracking! The Puppy Tracking Primer.* Wenatchee, WA: Dogwise Publishing, 2005.

Versatile Hunting Dog Training: Johnson, Chuck. *Training the Versatile Hunting Dog,* 2nd Edition. Belgrade, MT: Wilderness Adventures Press, 2009.

Behavior/Training

General Dog Behavior: Aloff, Brenda. *Canine Body Language, A Photographic Guide.* Wenatchee, WA: Dogwise Publishing, 2005.

Coren, Stanley. *How Dogs Think: What the World Looks Like to Them and Why They Act the Way They Do.* New York: Simon & Schuster, 2005.

Donaldson, Jean. *Oh Behave! Dogs from Pavlov to Premack to Pinker.* Wenatchee, WA: Dogwise Publishing, 2008.

McConnell, PhD, Patricia B. *For the Love of a Dog: Understanding Emotion in You and Your Best Friend.* New York: Random House, 2006.

Behavior (Problem): Donaldson, Jean. *Mine! A Guide to Resource Guarding in Dogs.* San Francisco: Kinship Communications/SF-SPCA, 2002.

Killion, Jane. *When Pigs Fly: Training Success with Impossible Dogs.* Wenatchee, WA: Dogwise Publishing, 2007.

McConnell, PhD, Patricia B. *I'll Be Home Soon! How to Prevent and Treat Separation Anxiety.* Black Earth, WI: Dog's Best Friend, 2000.

McConnell, PhD, Patricia B., and Karen B. London, PhD. *The Feisty Fido: Help for the Leash-Aggressive Dog.* Black Earth, WI: Dog's Best Friend, 2003.

Pryor, Karen. *Don't Shoot the Dog! The New Art of Teaching and Training.* Waltham, MA: Sunshine Books, 2006.

Housetraining: Palika, Liz. *The Pocket Idiot's Guide to Housetraining Your Dog.* New York: Penguin Group (USA), 2007.

Socializing with Dogs: Bennett, Robin, and Susan Briggs. *Off-leash Dog Play: A Complete Guide to Safety and Fun.* Woodbridge, VA: C&R Publishing, 2008.

McConnell, Patricia B. *Feeling Outnumbered? How to Manage and Enjoy Your Multi-dog Household* (expanded and updated edition). Black Earth, WI: Dog's Best Friend, 2008.

Socializing with People: Long, Lorie. *A Dog Who's Always Welcome: Assistance and Therapy Dog Trainers Teach You How to Socialize and Train Your Companion Dog.* New York: John Wiley & Sons, 2008.

McConnell, Patricia B. *How to Be the Leader of the Pack and Have Your Dog Love You for It!* Black Earth, WI: Dog's Best Friend, 1996.

Index

175